"That love is inexhaustible, you will be there"
forever

THIS BOOK
Belongs to

Visit Our Author Page At

amazon.com

Scan me

Black Rose PRESS HOUSE

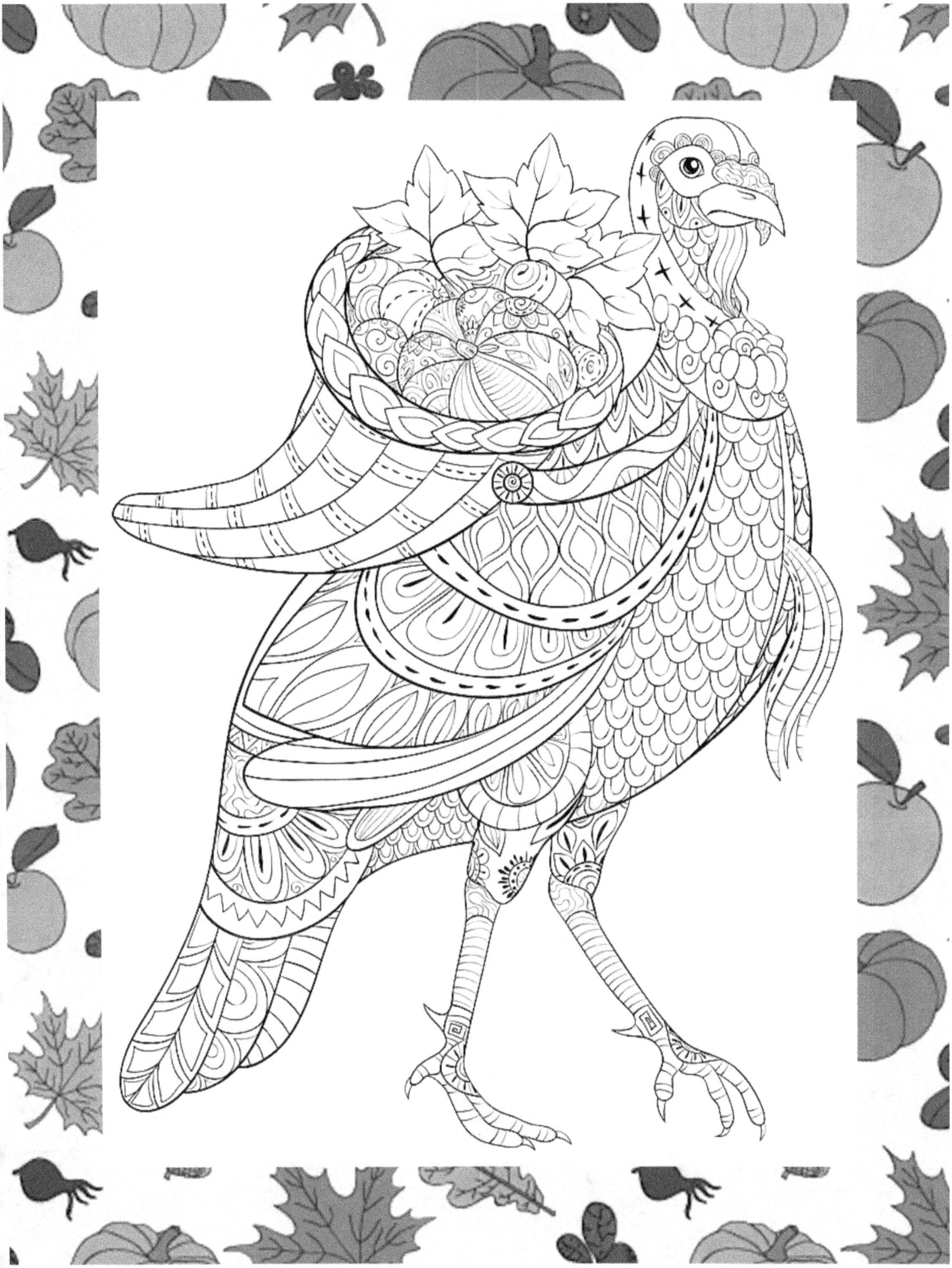

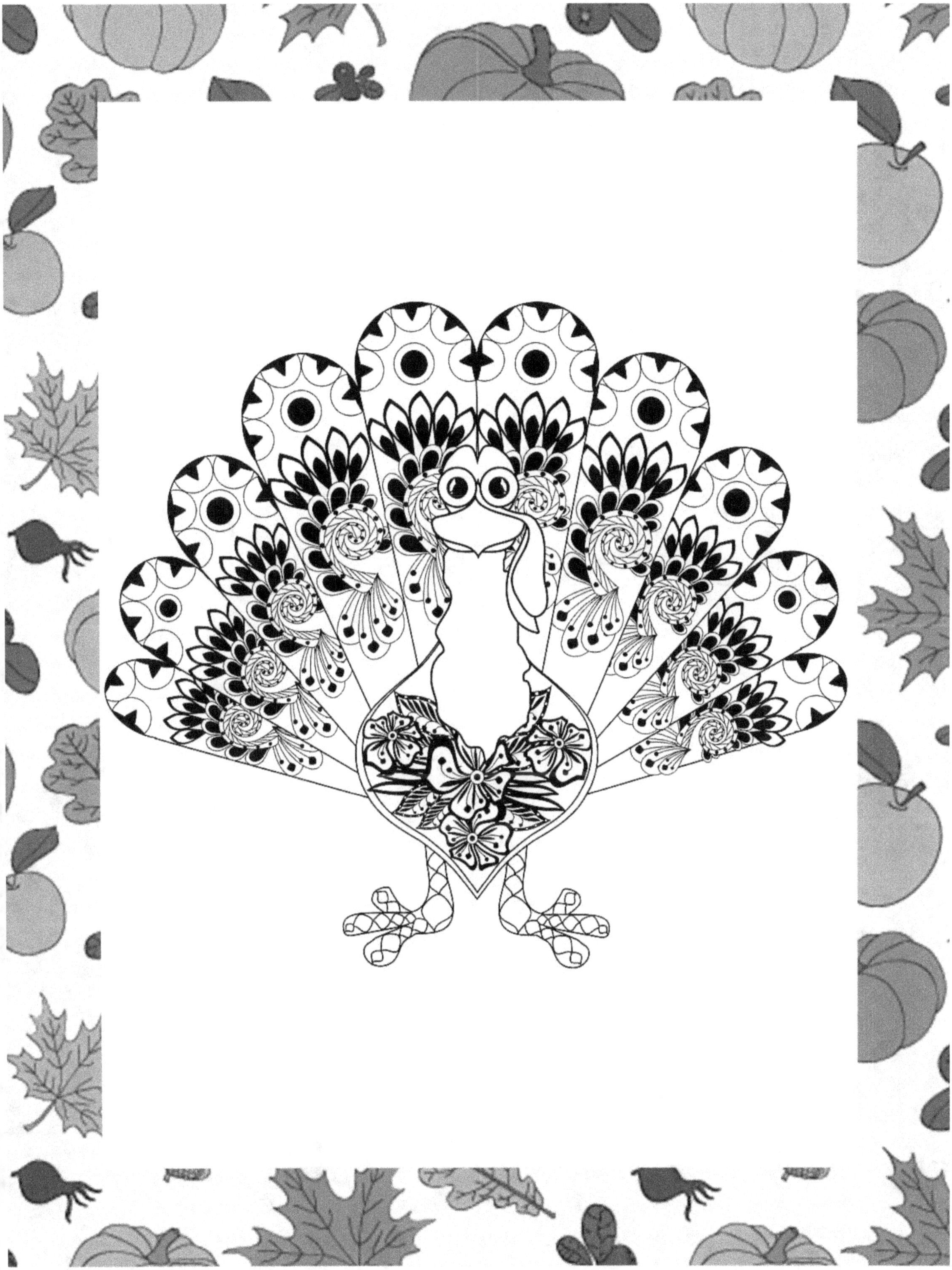

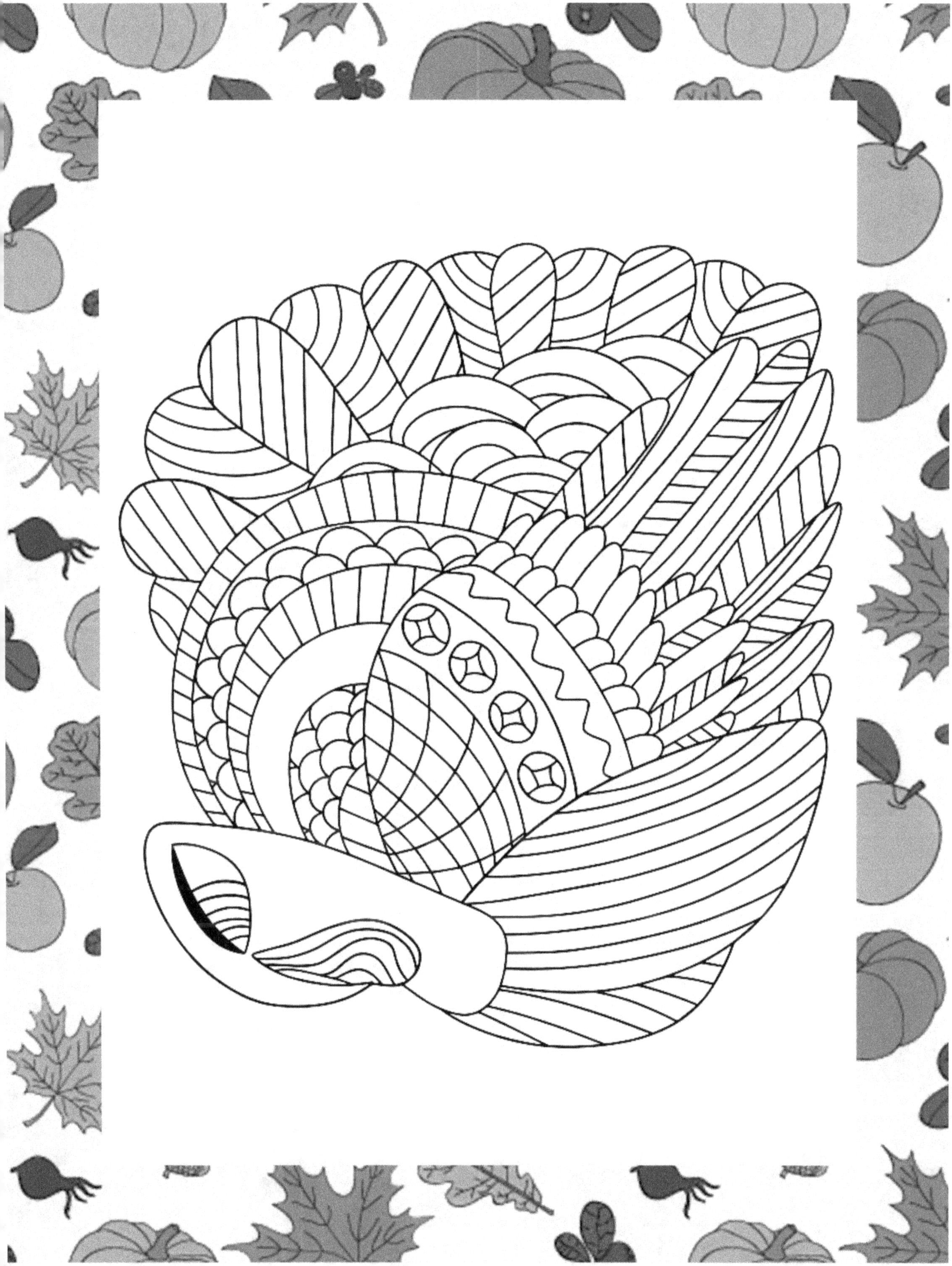

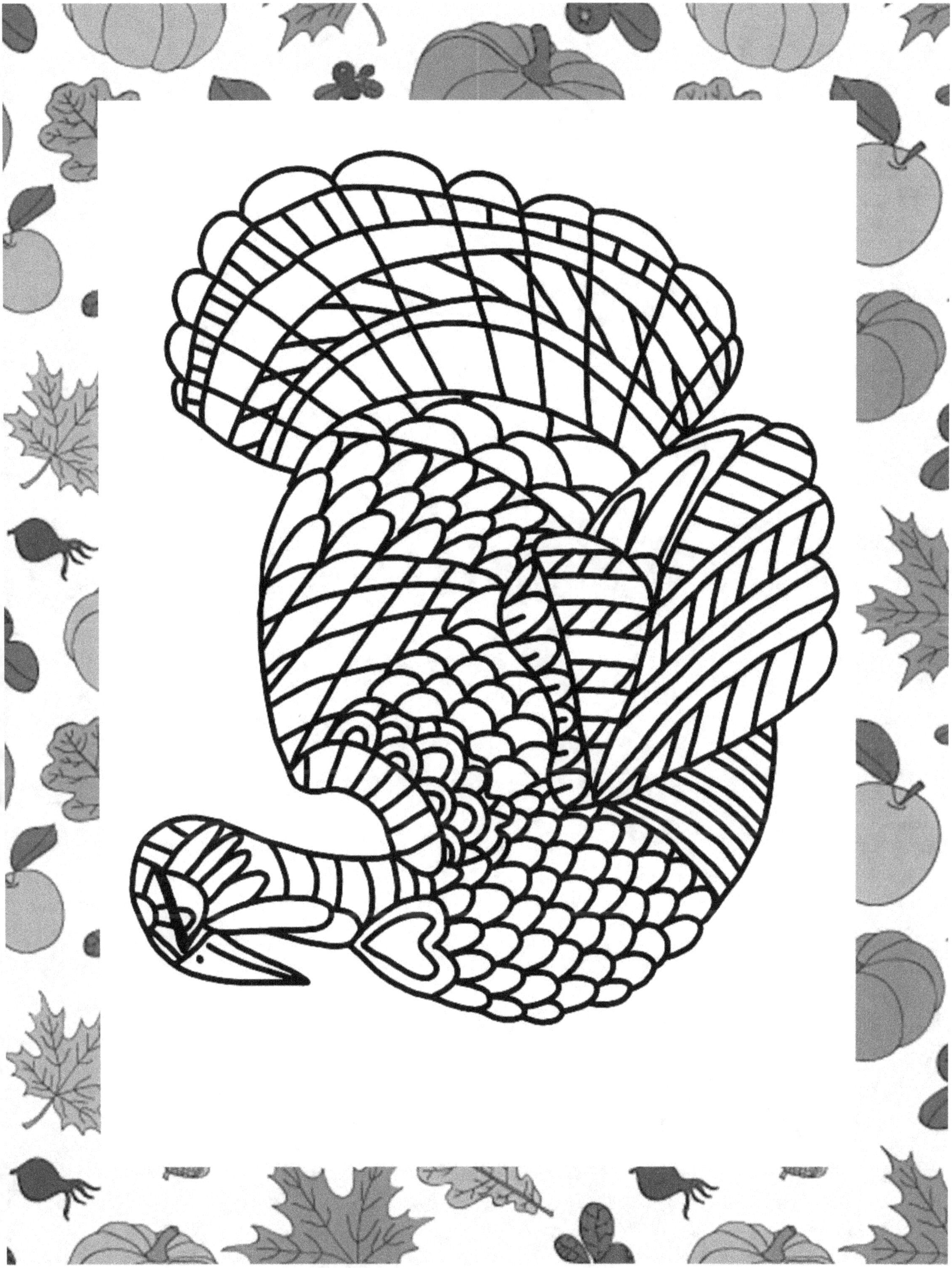

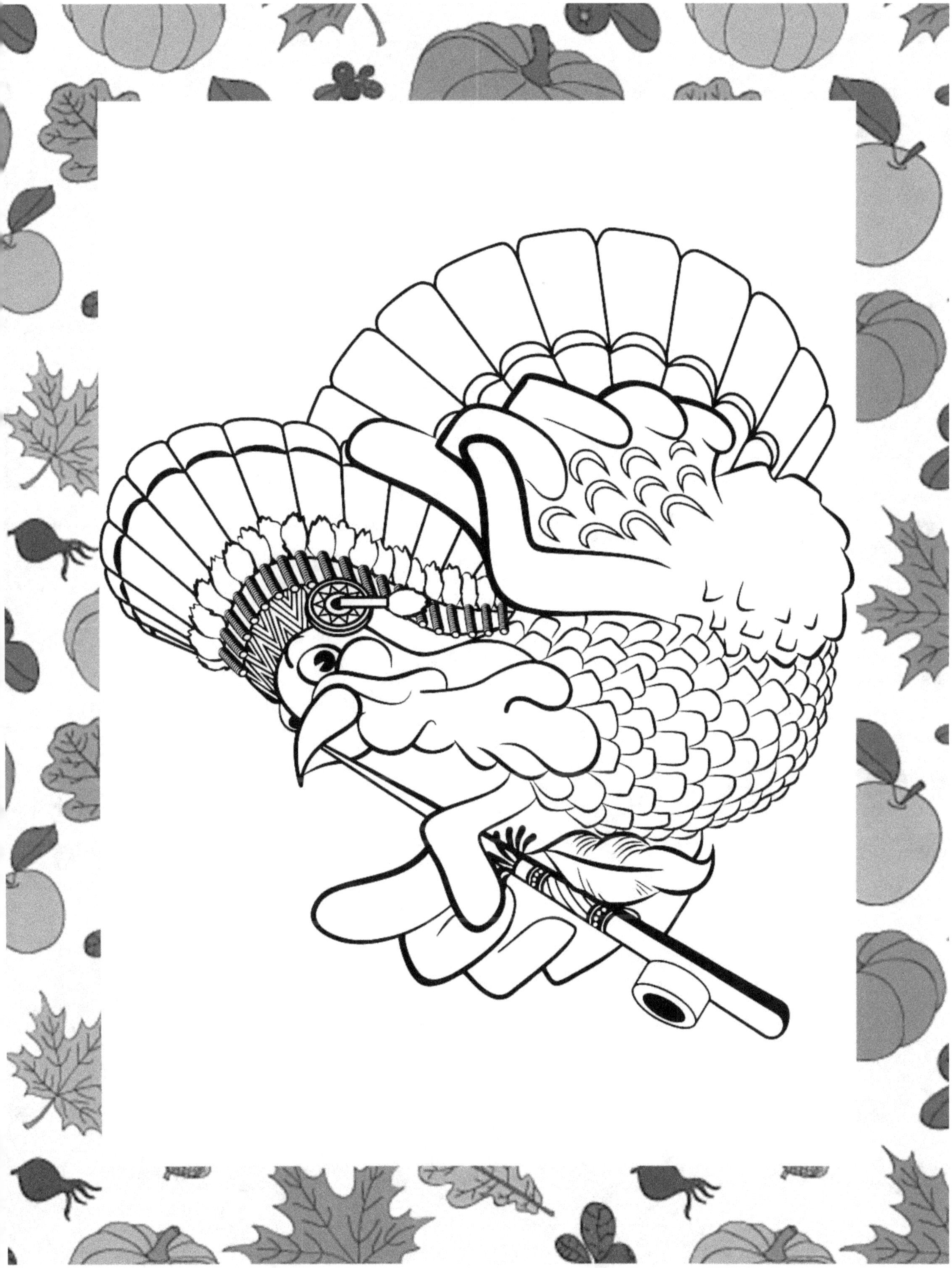

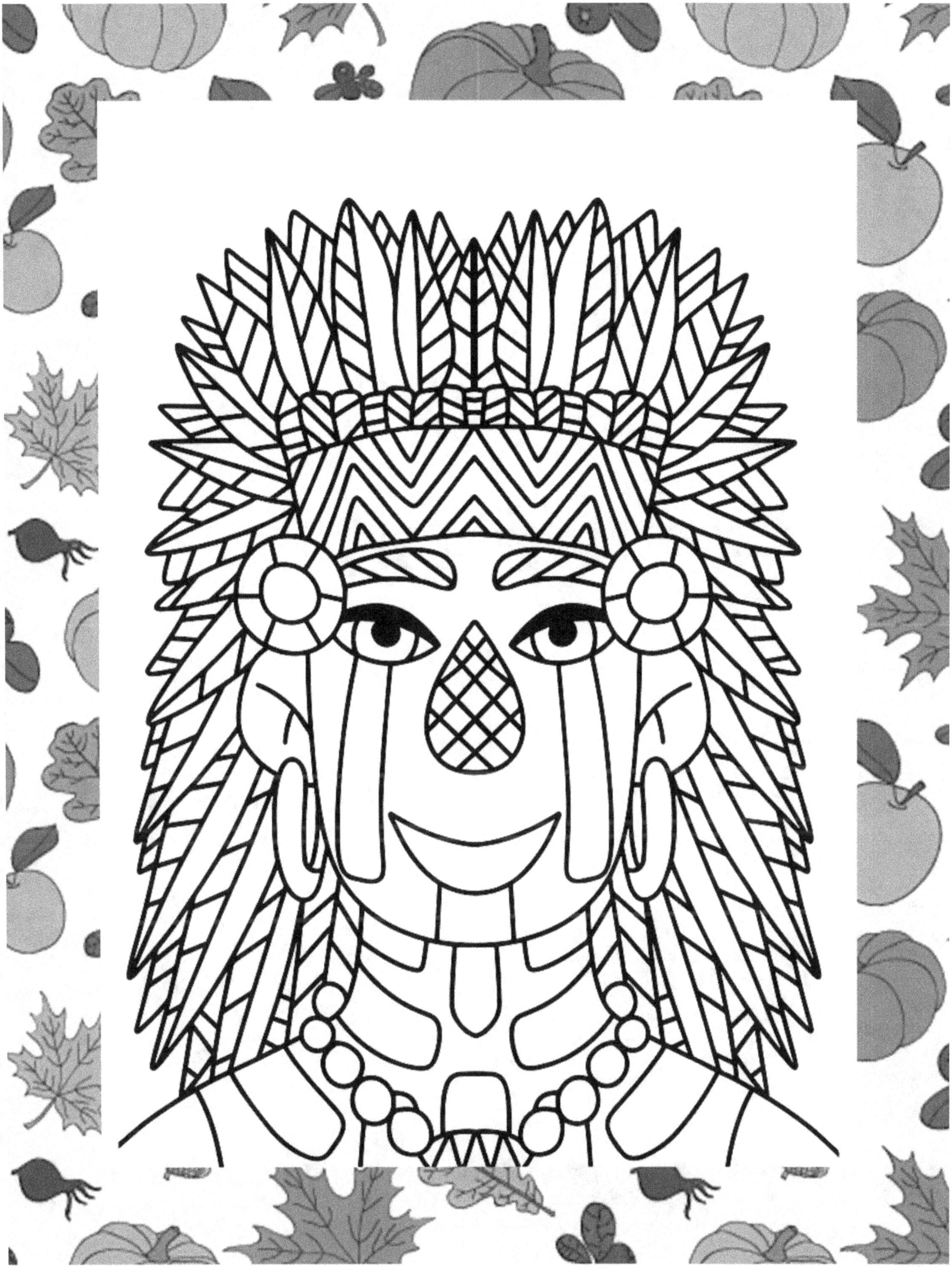

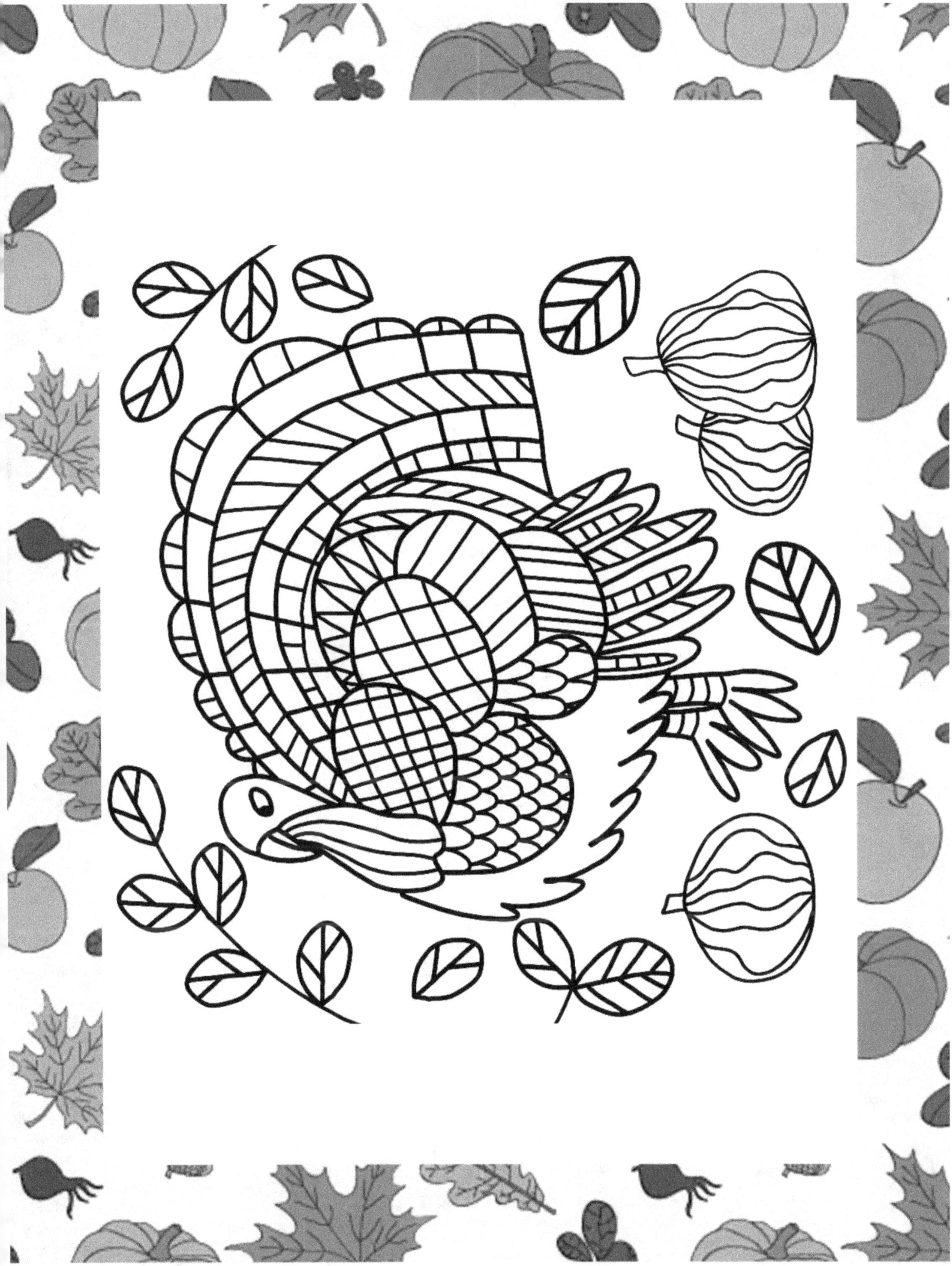

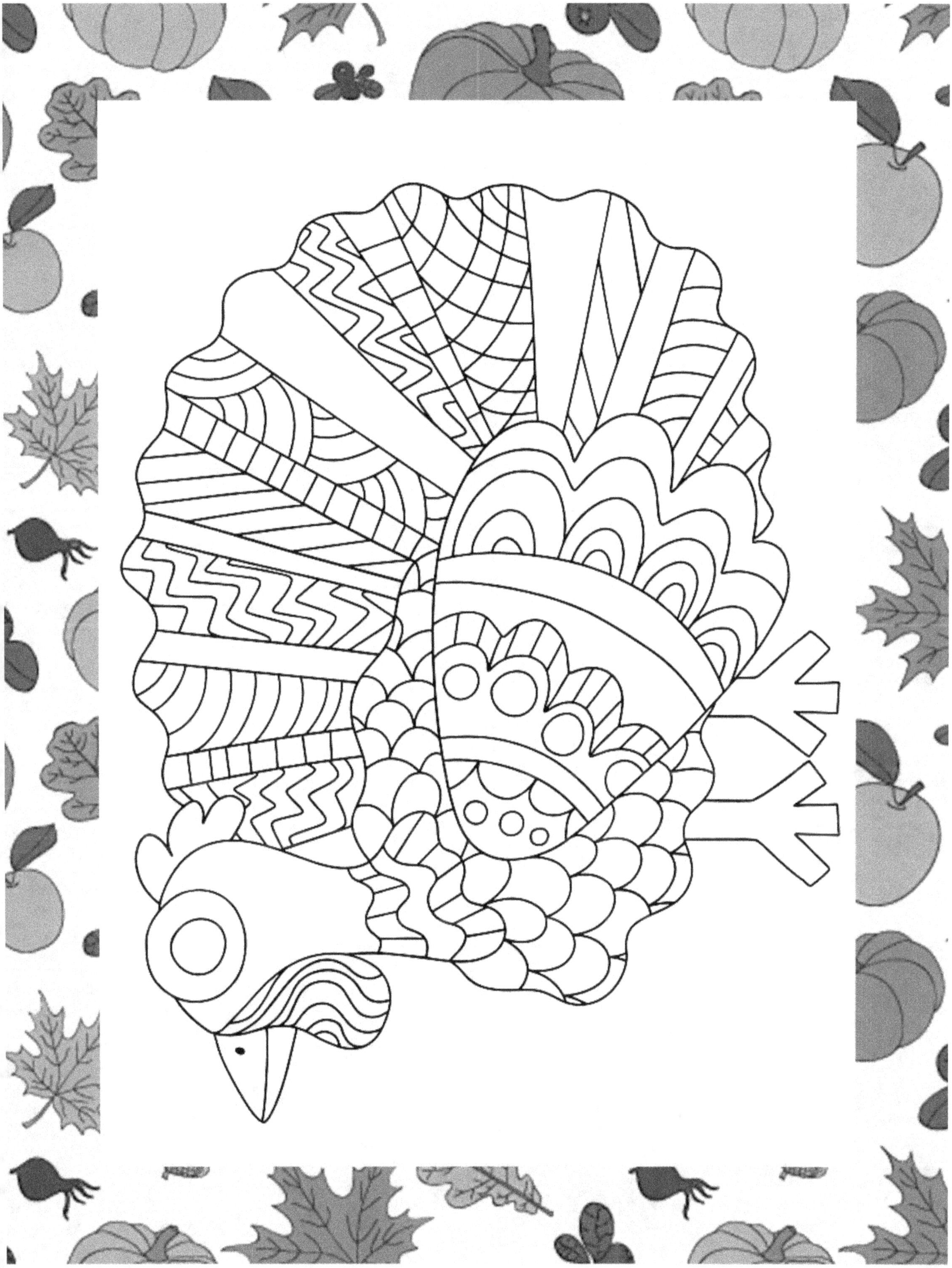

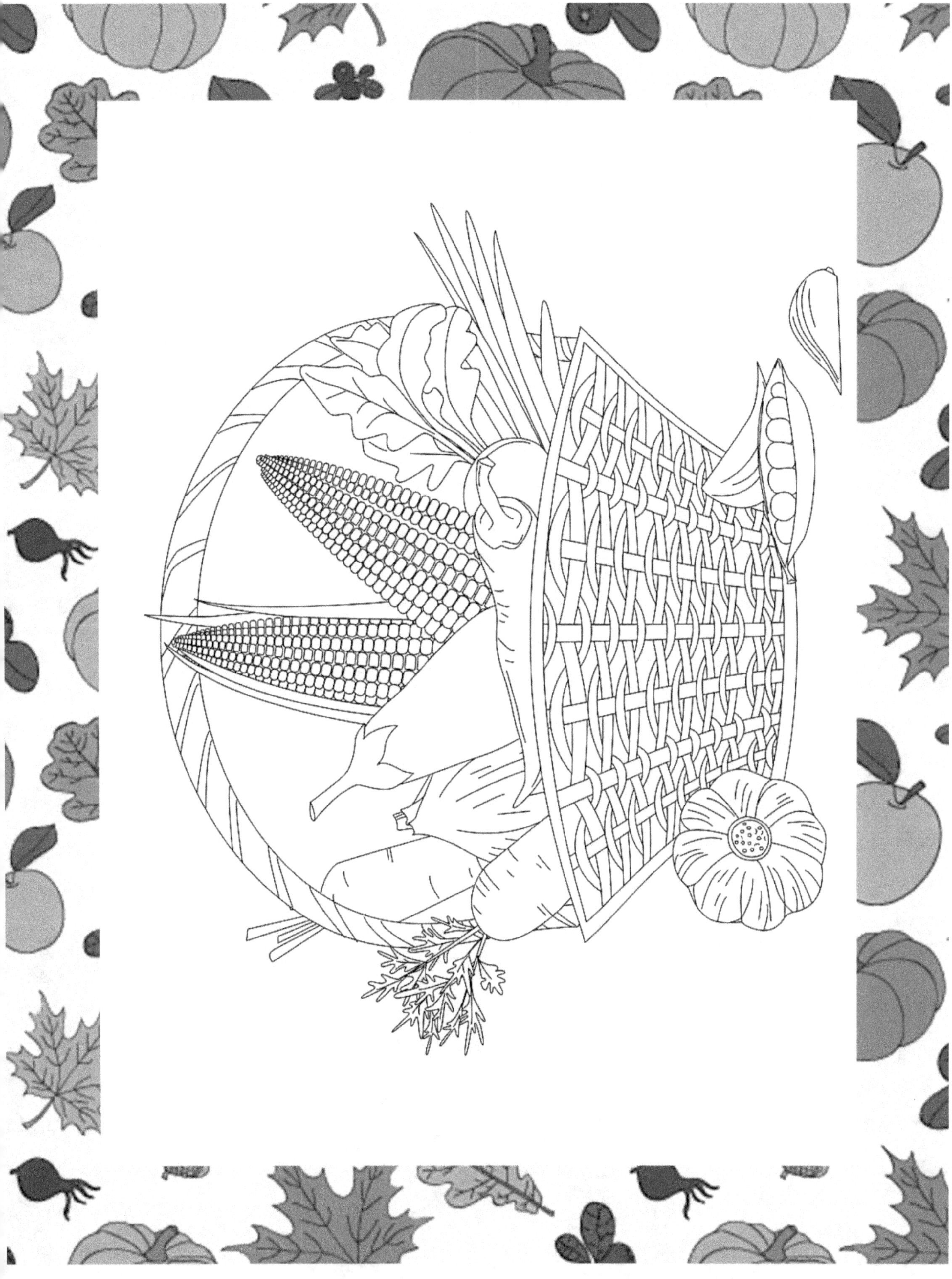

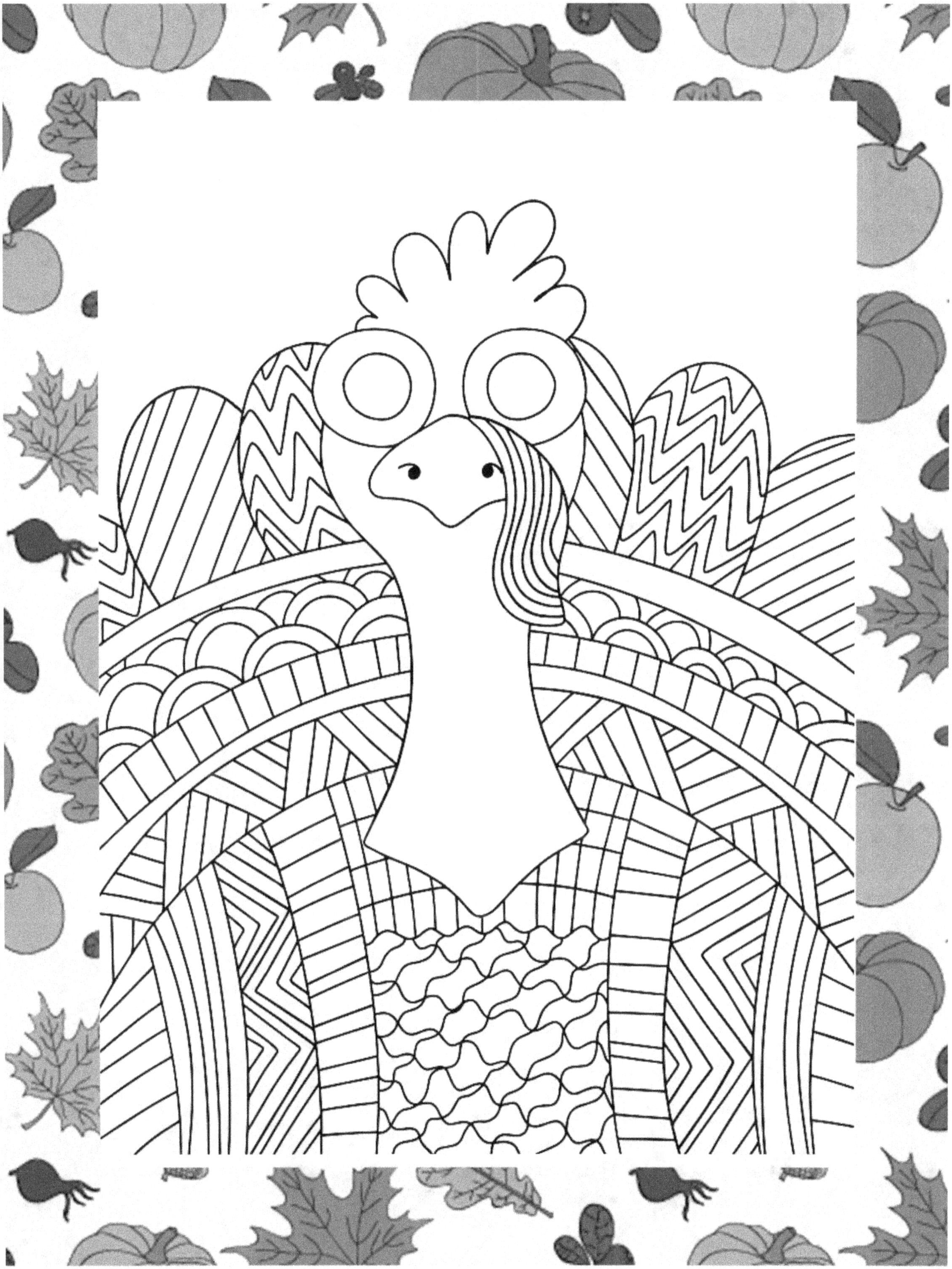

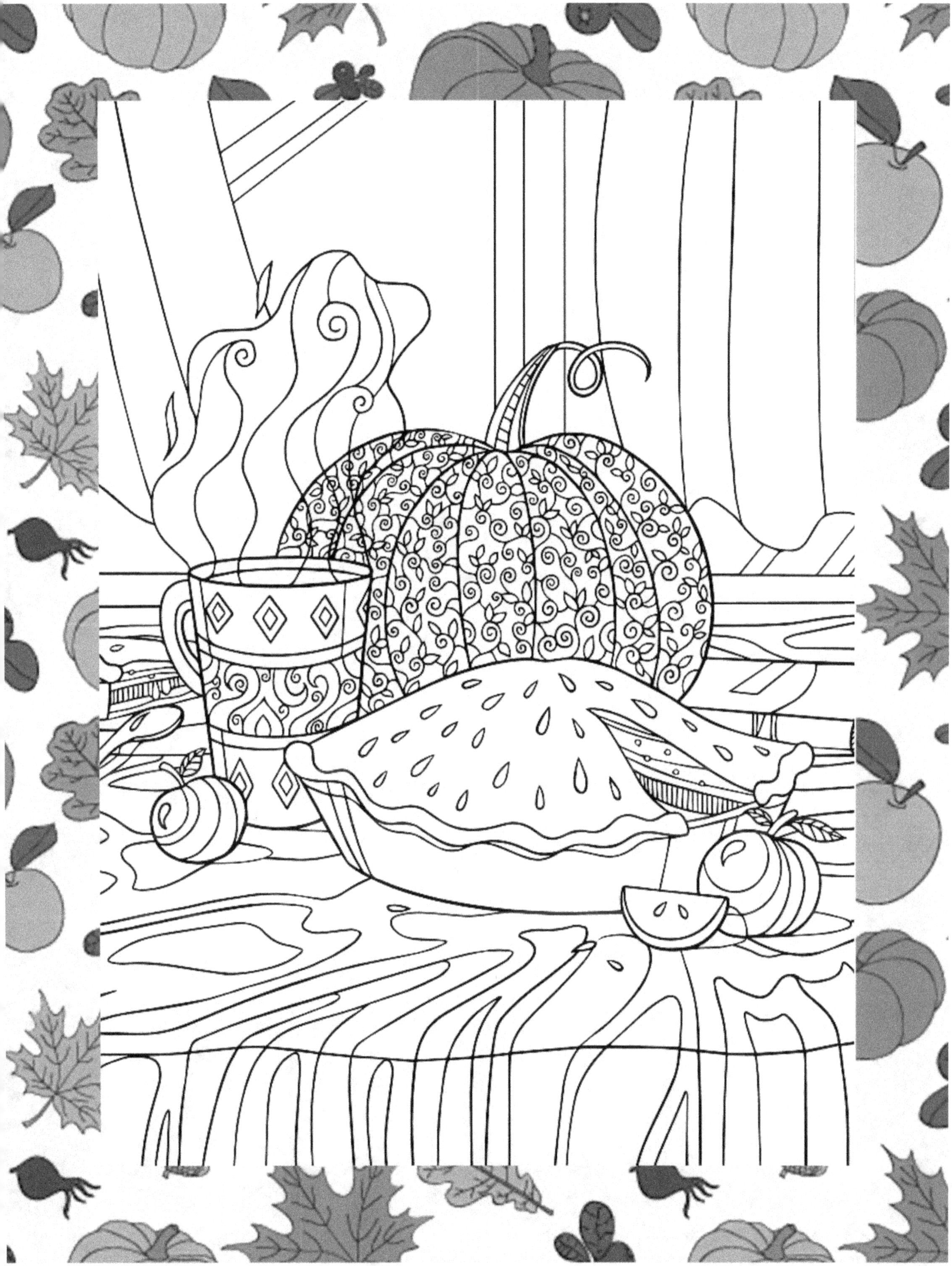

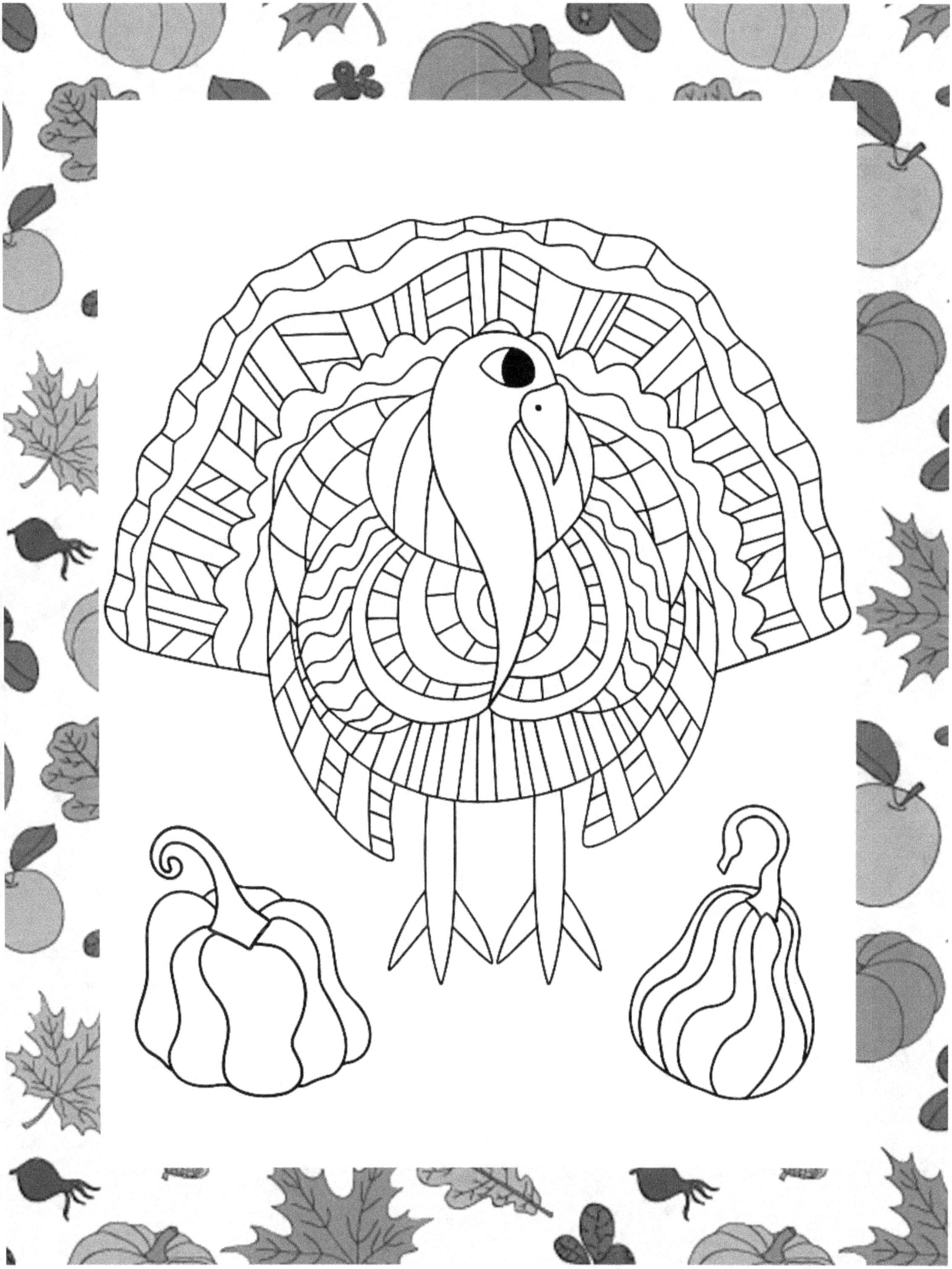

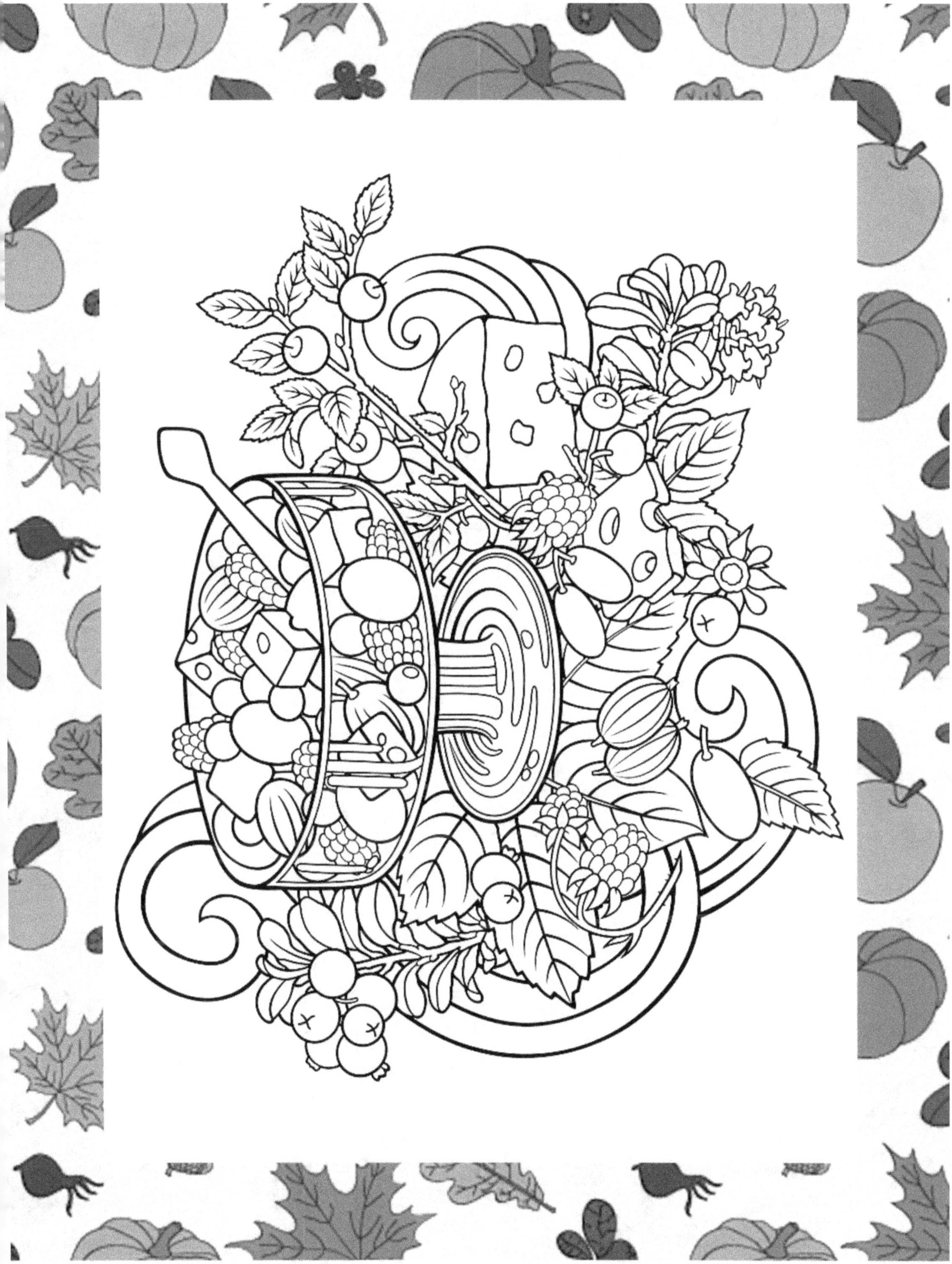

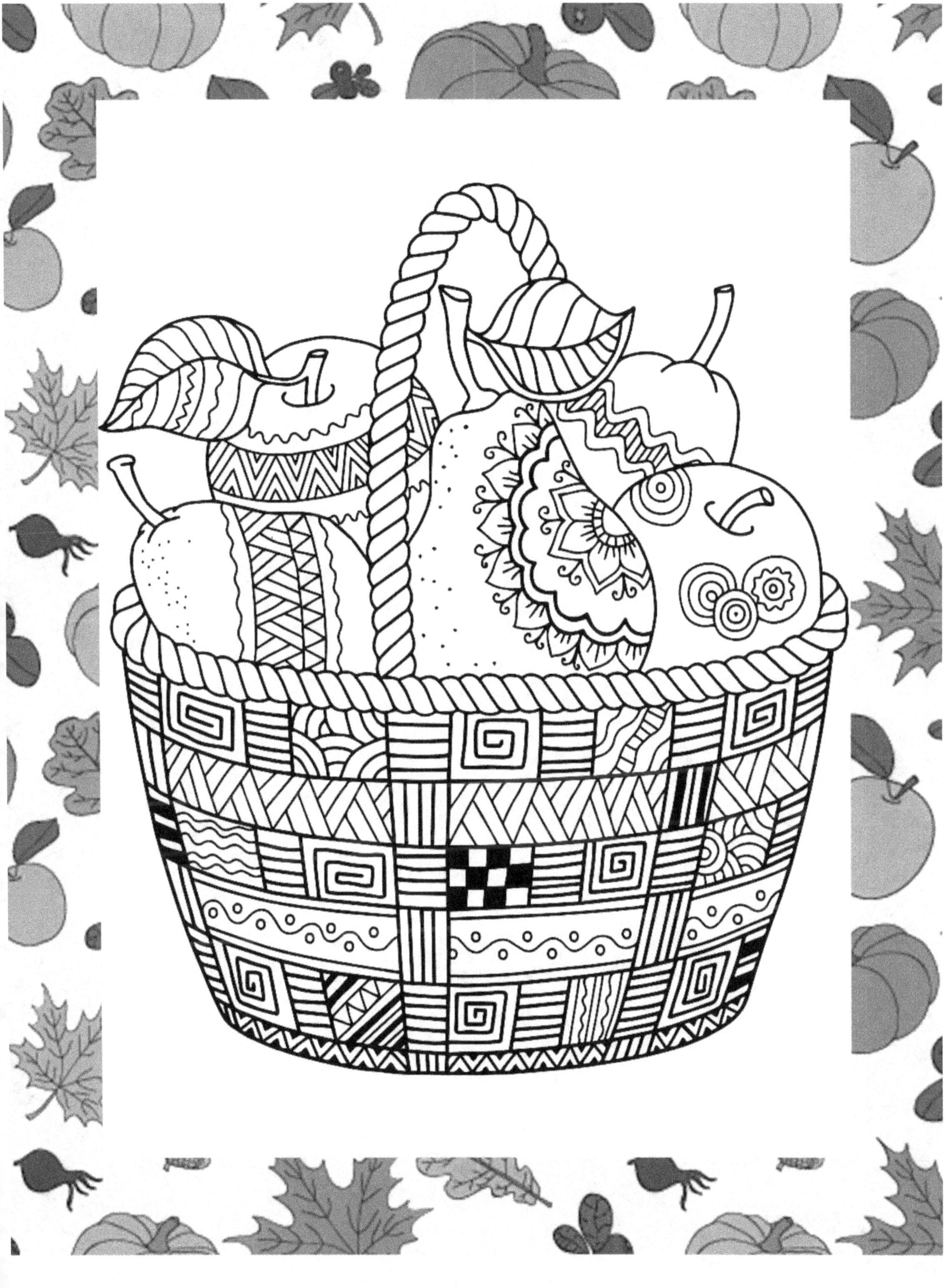

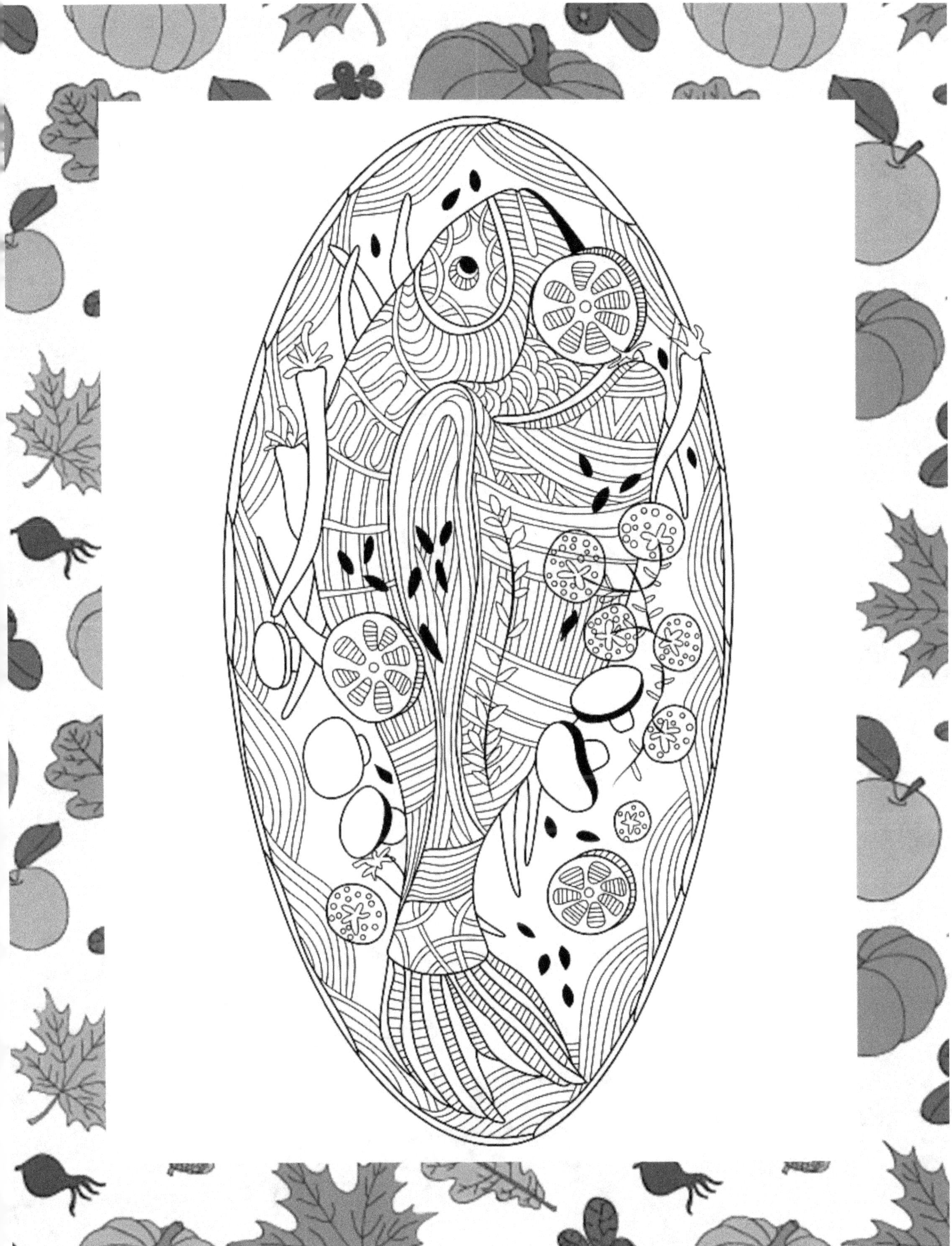

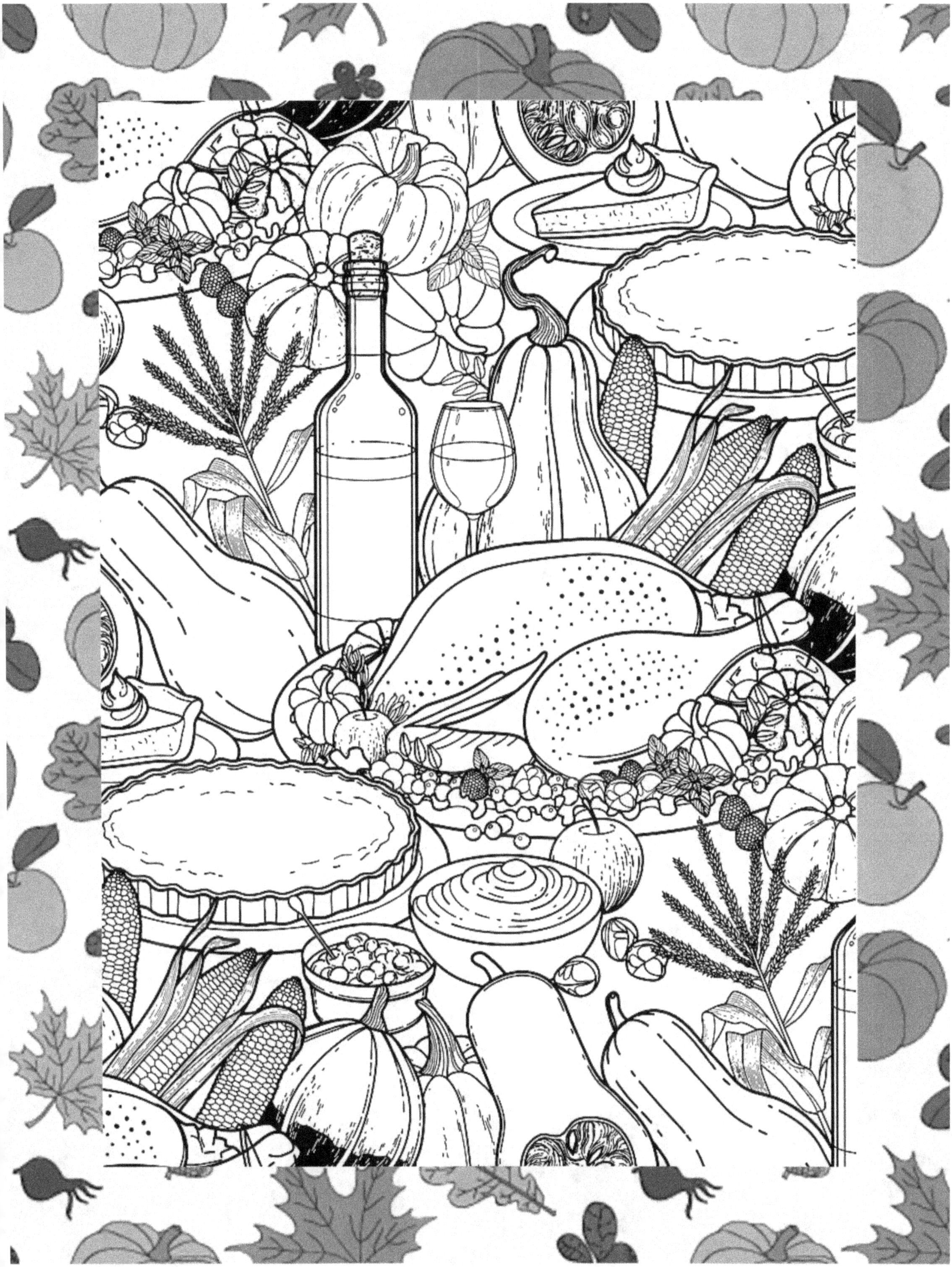

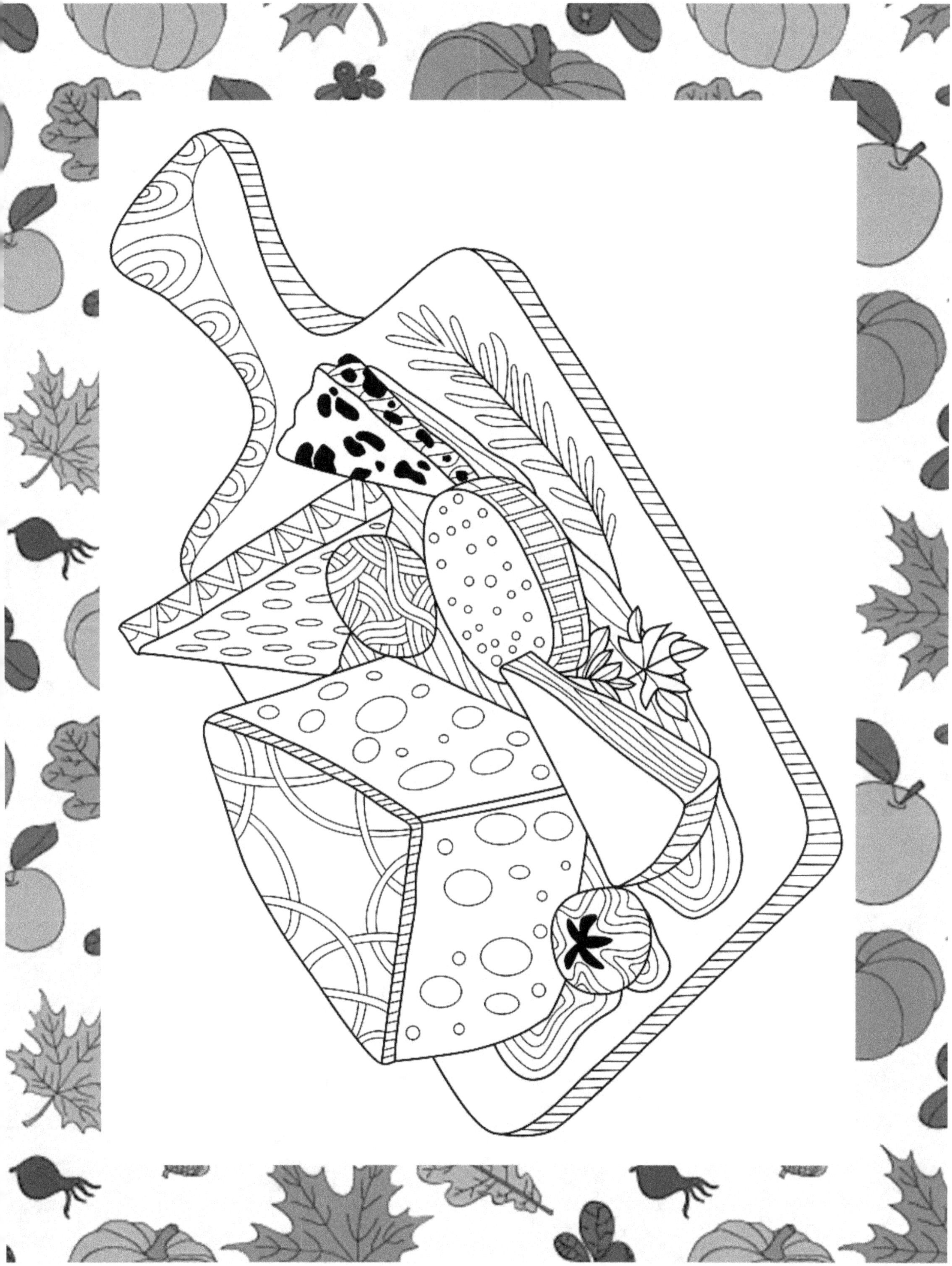

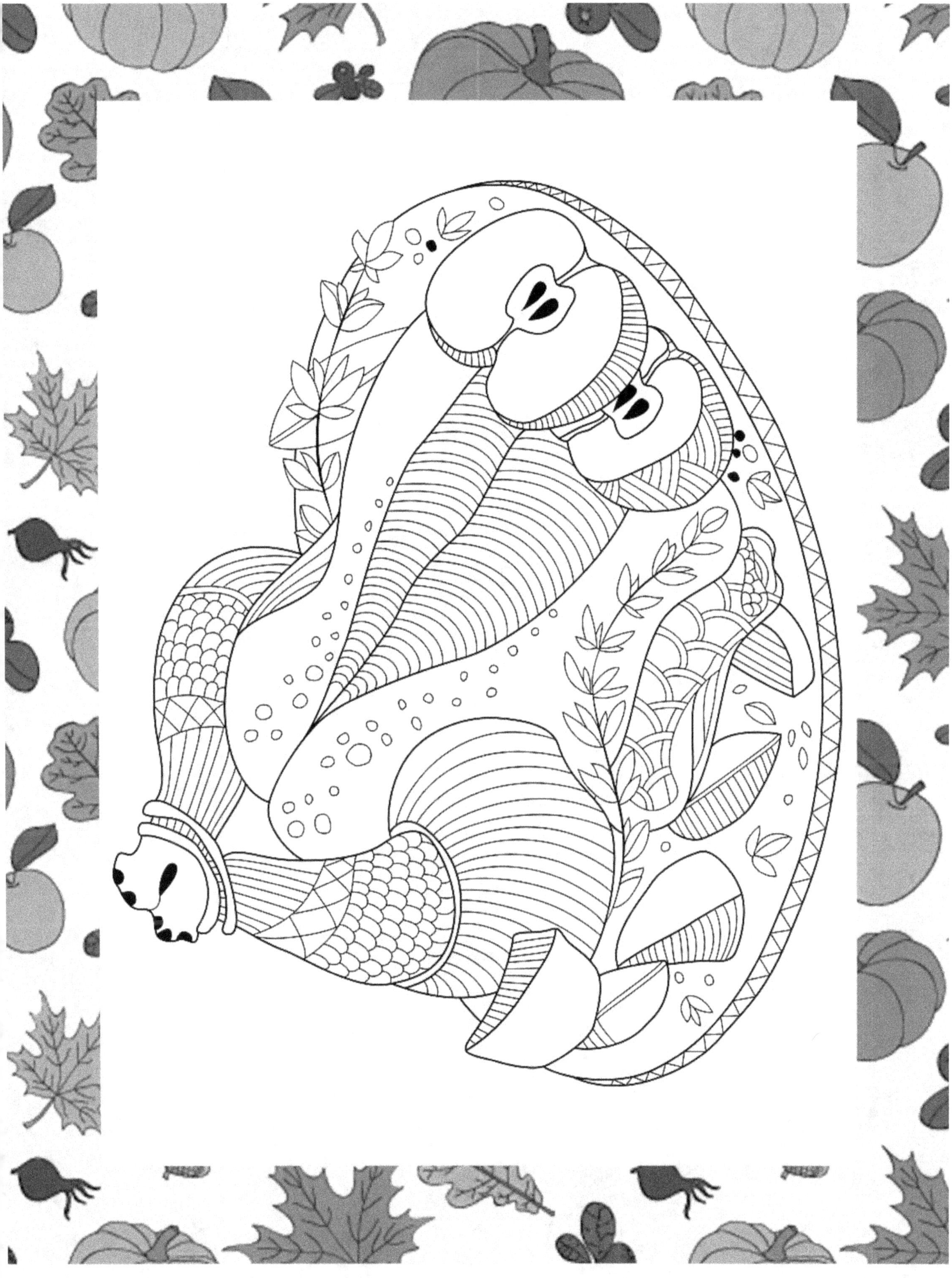

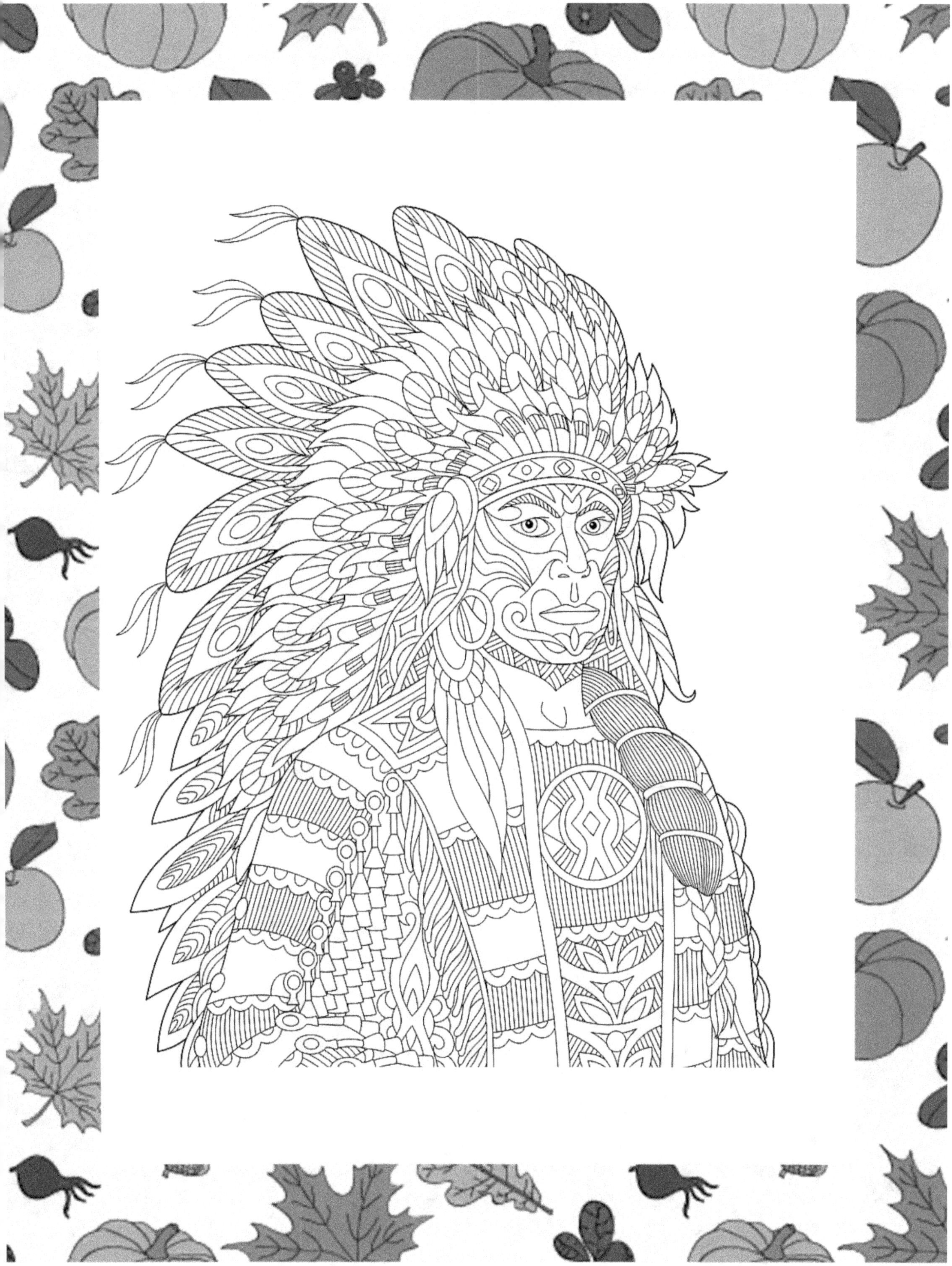

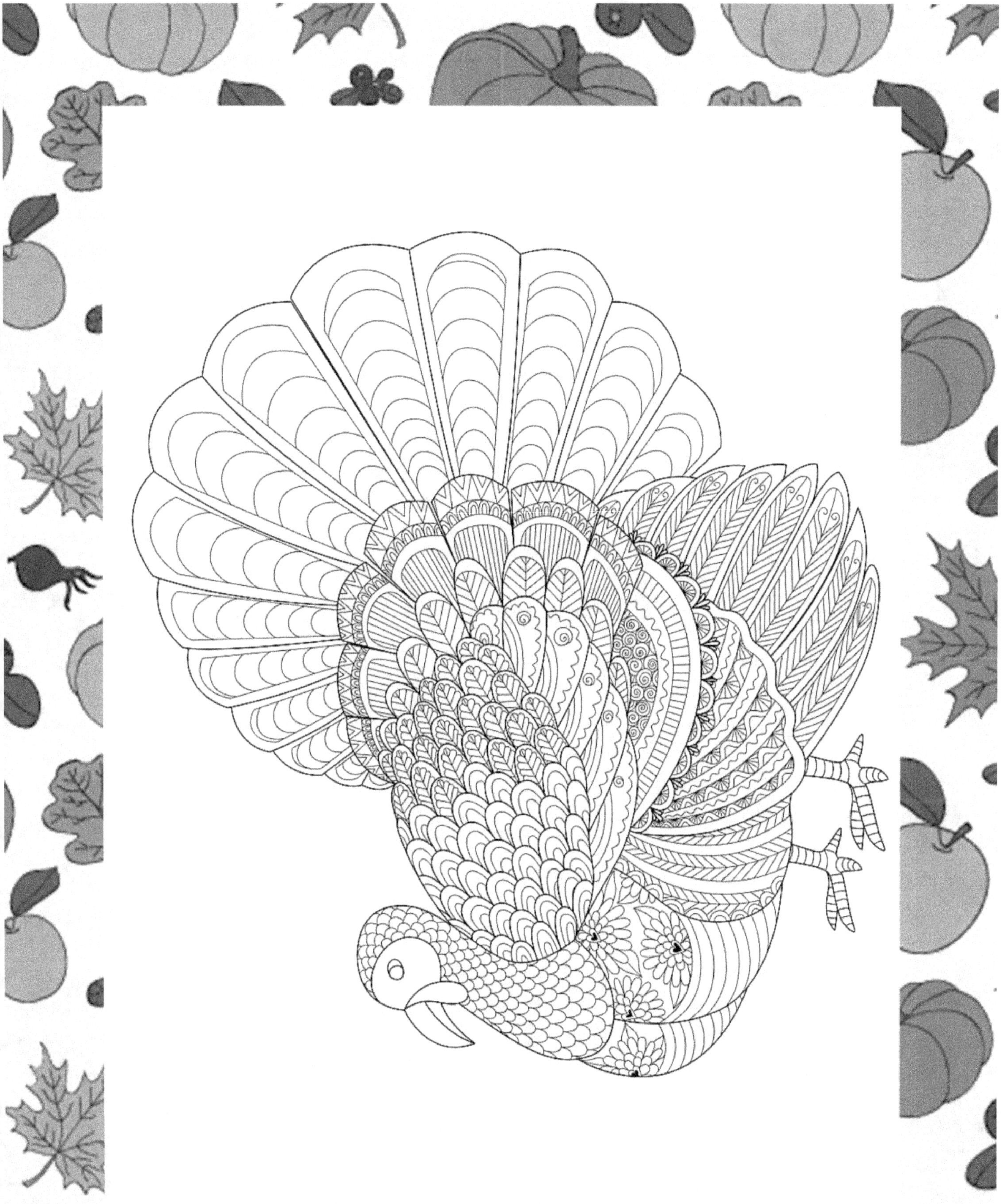

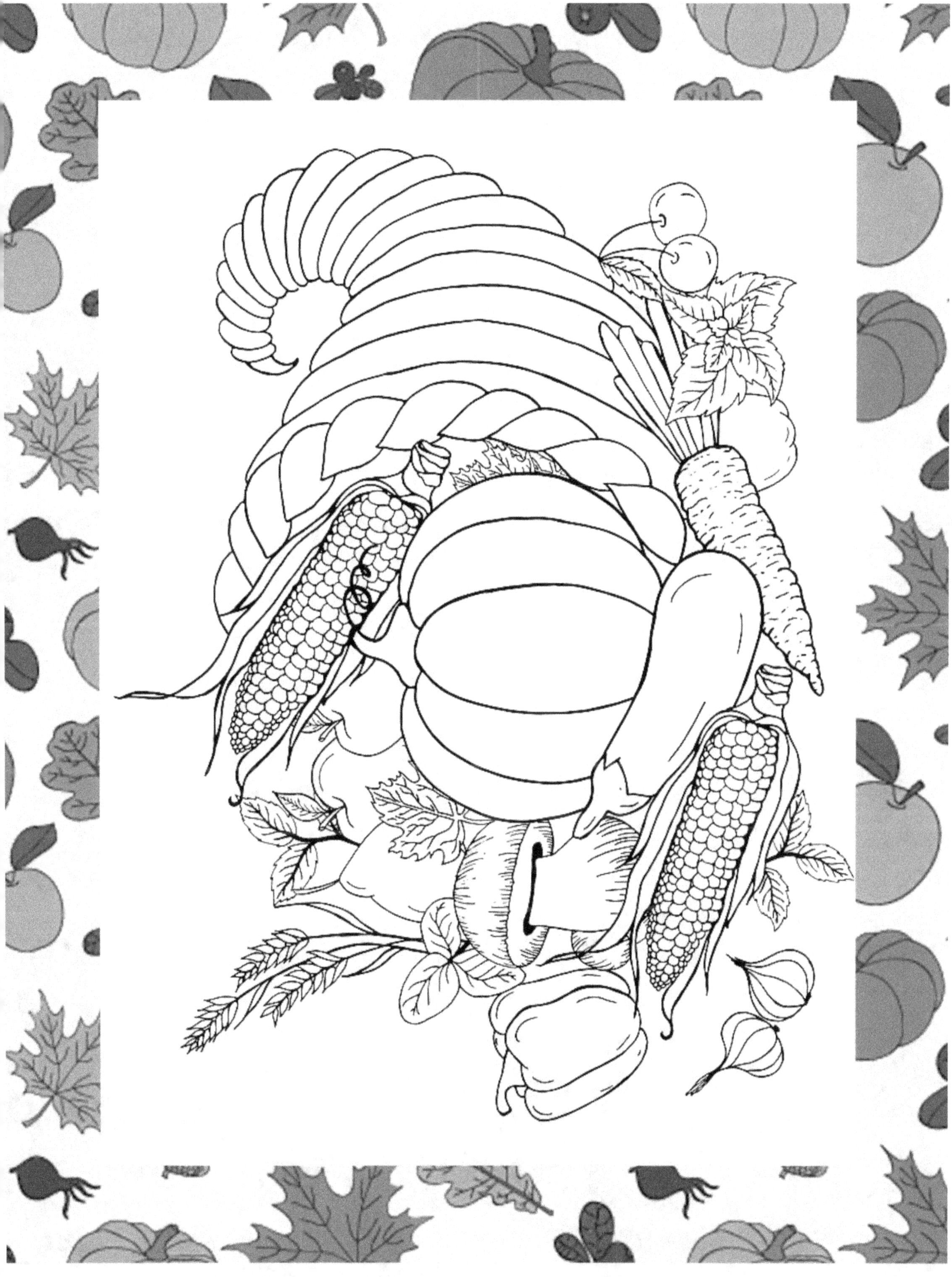

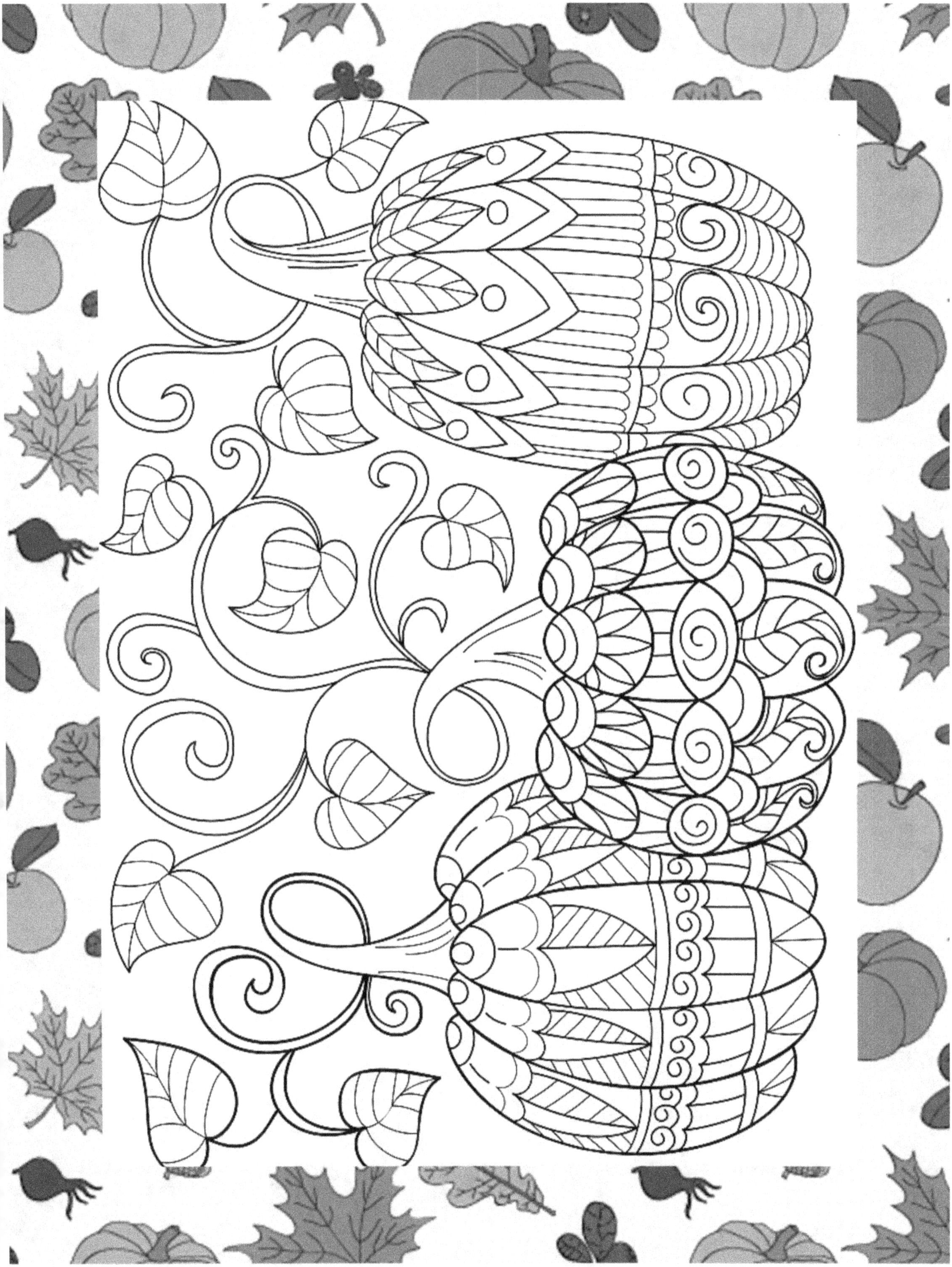

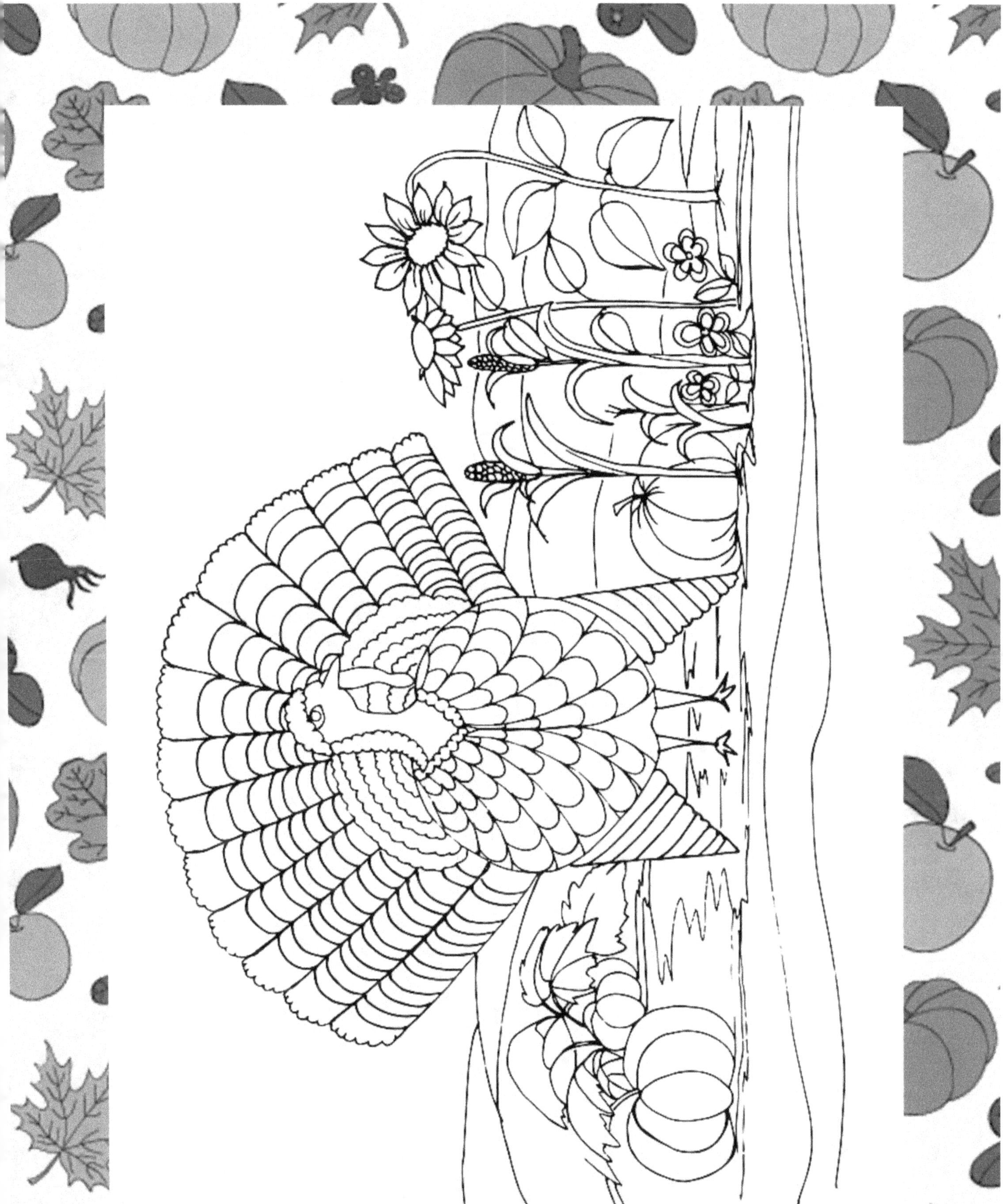

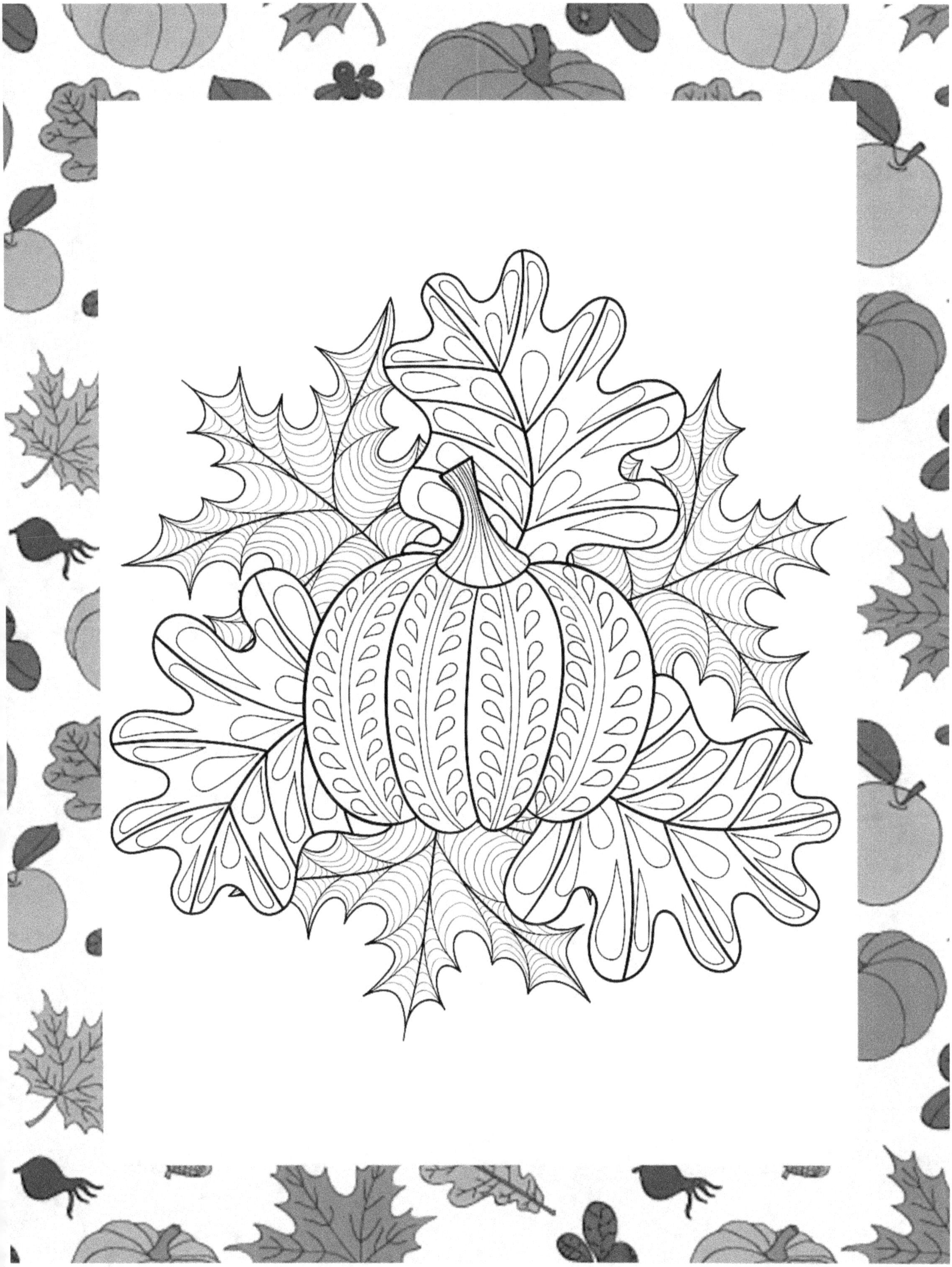

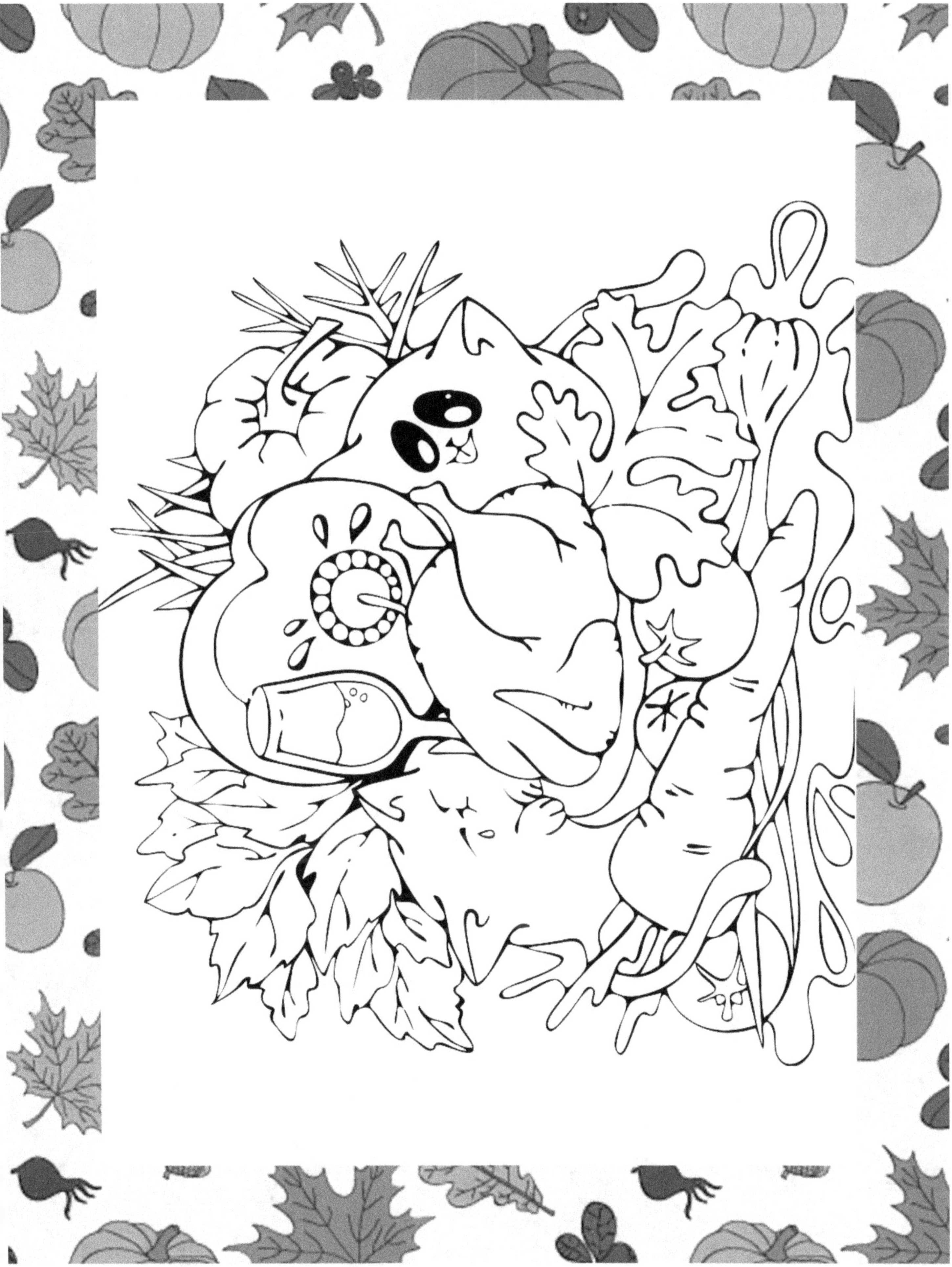

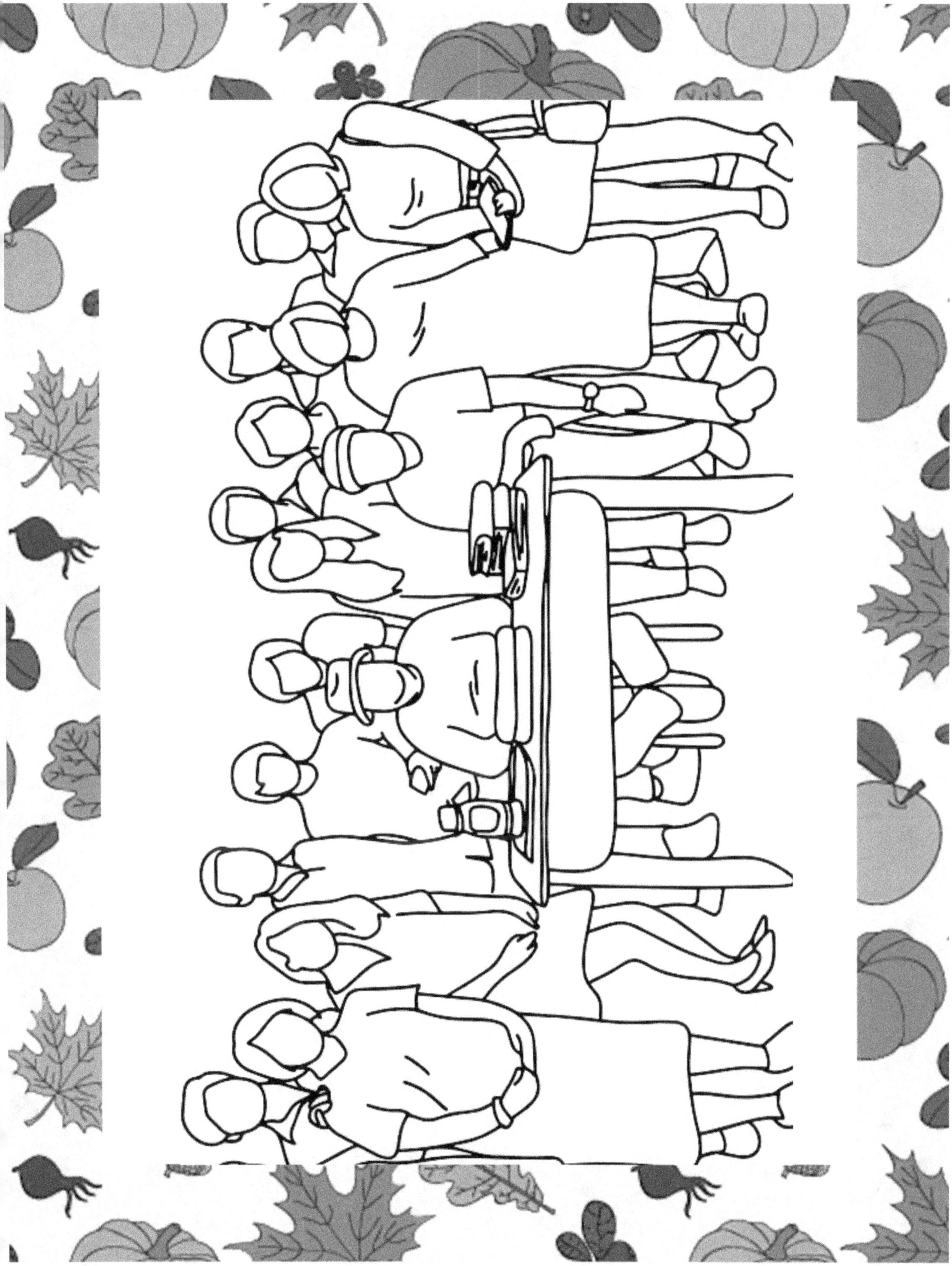

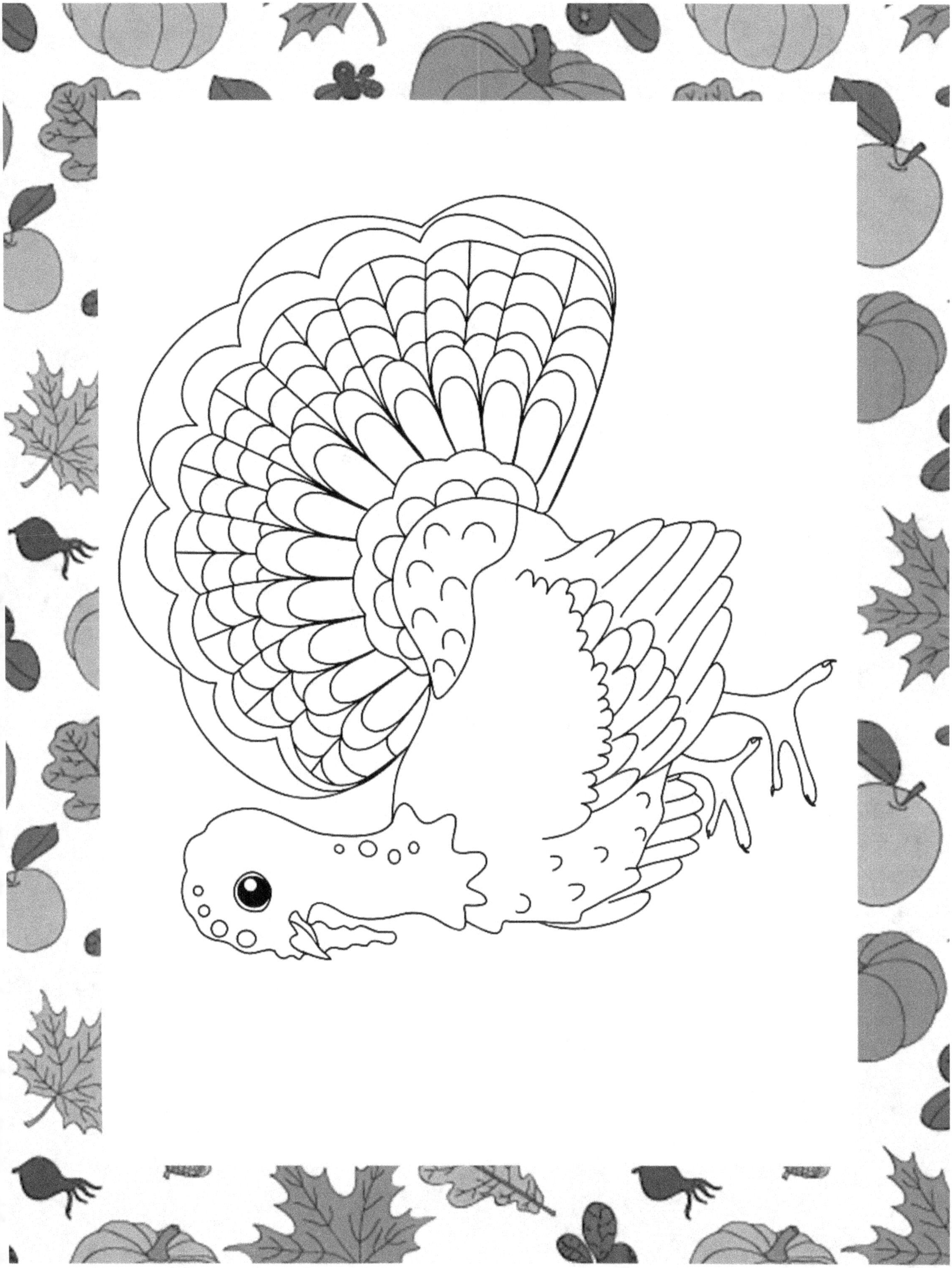

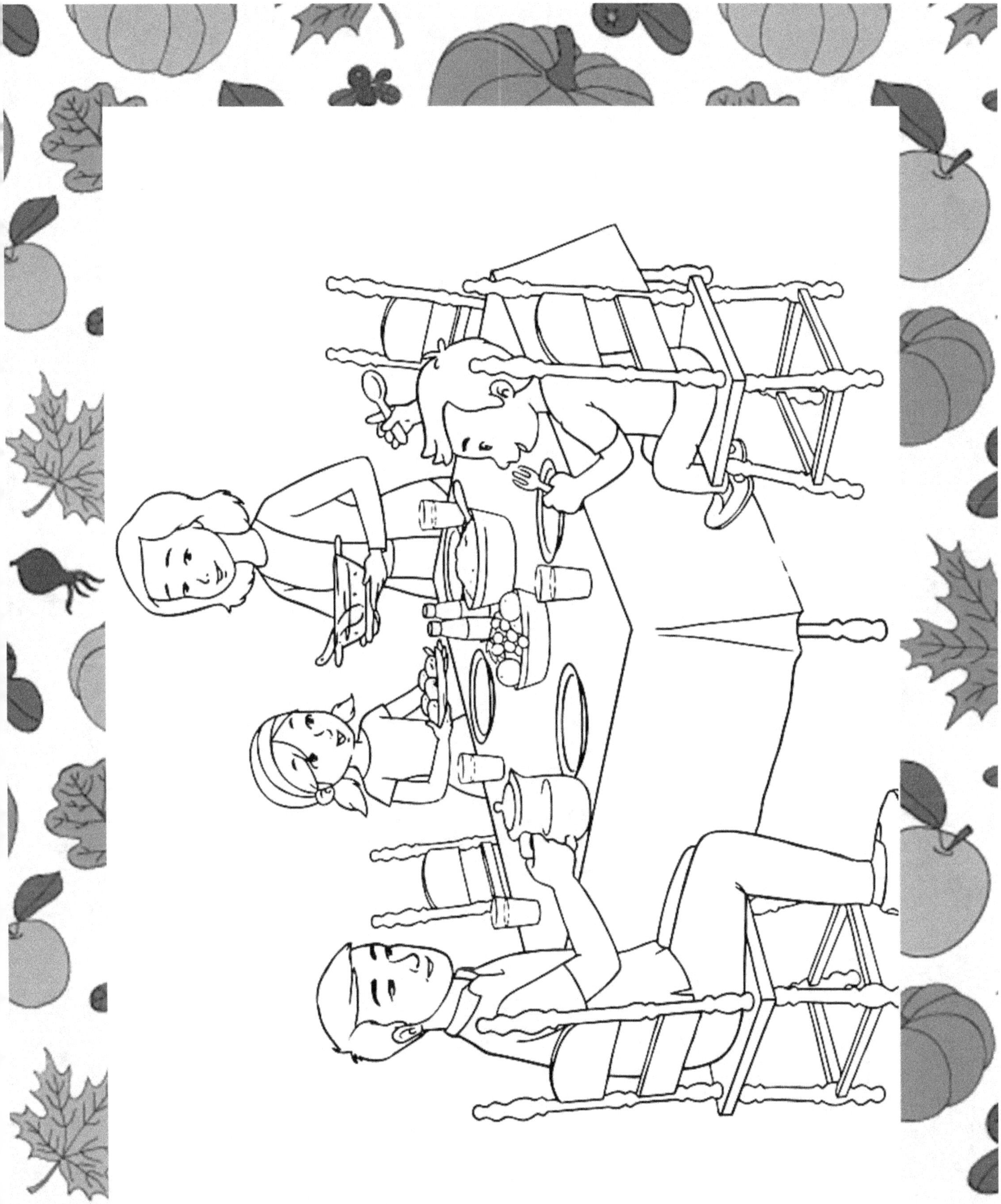

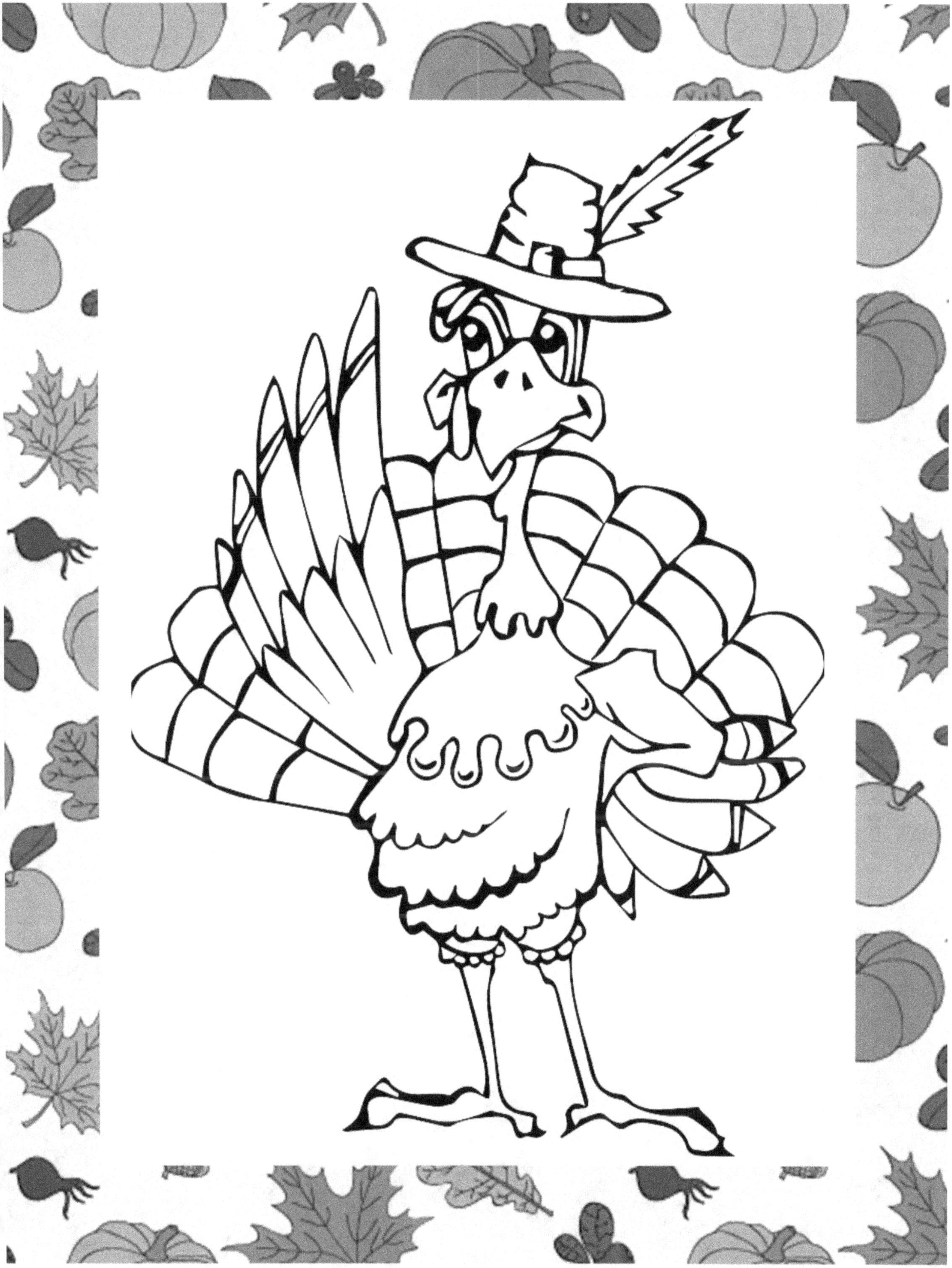

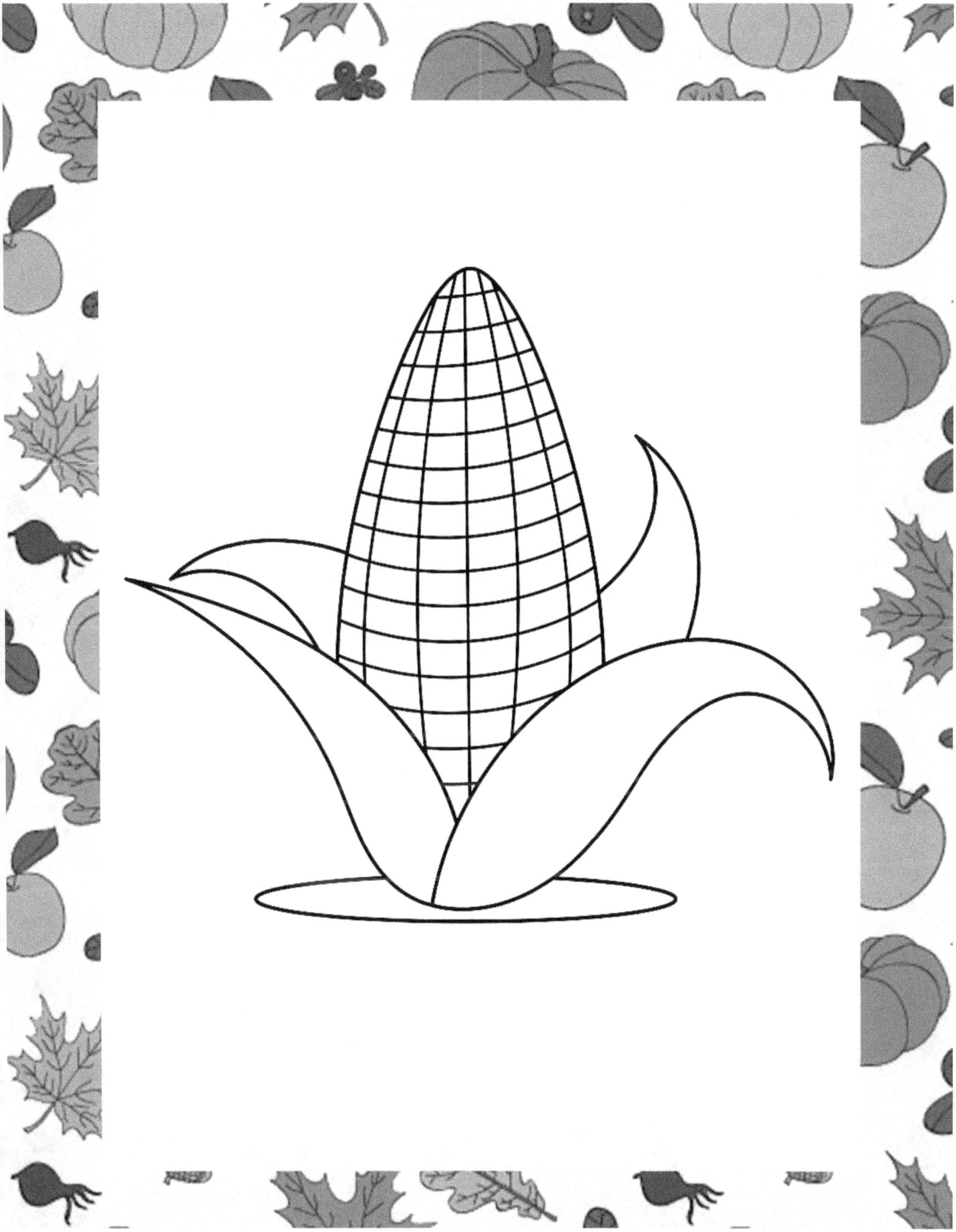

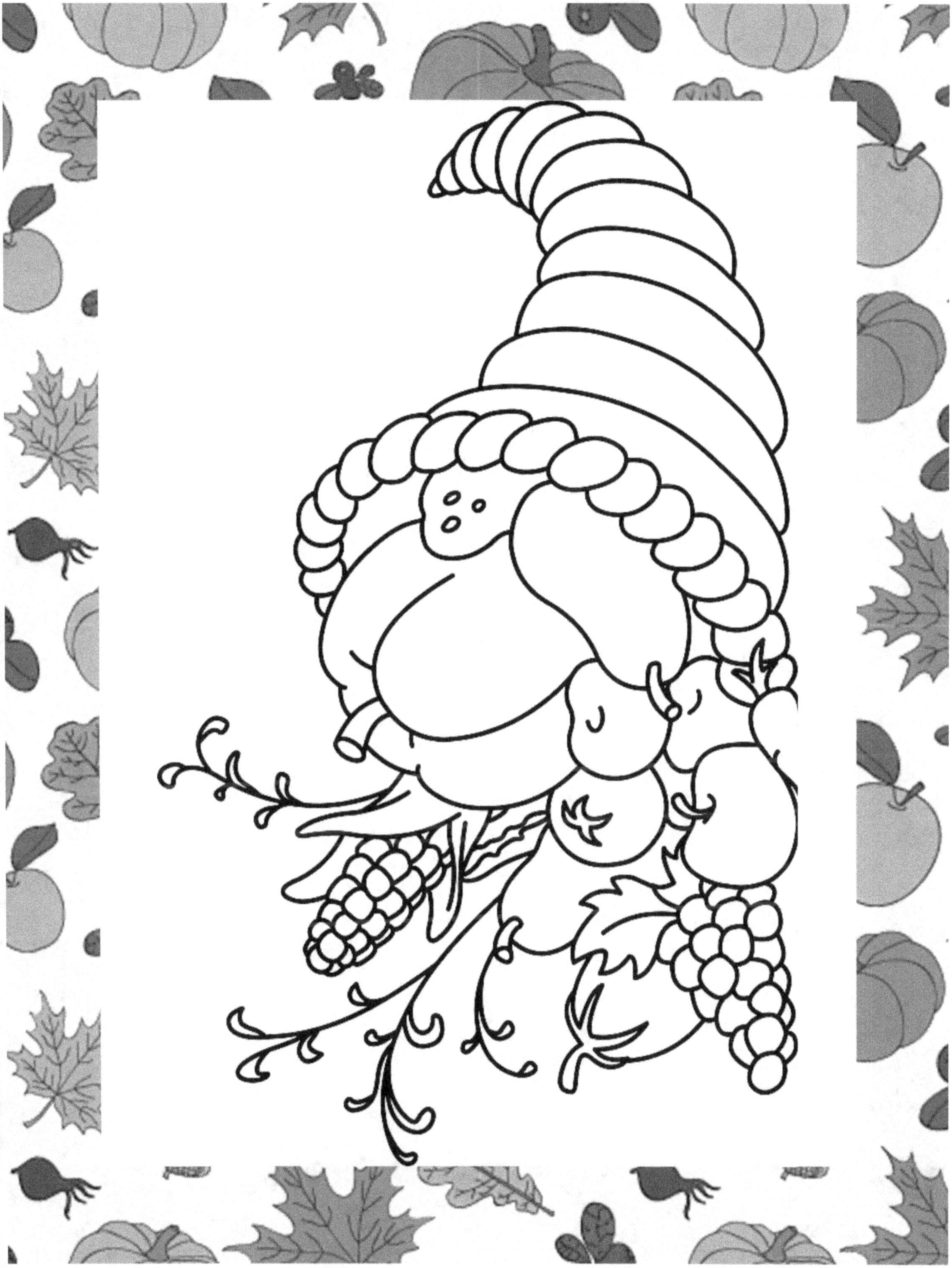

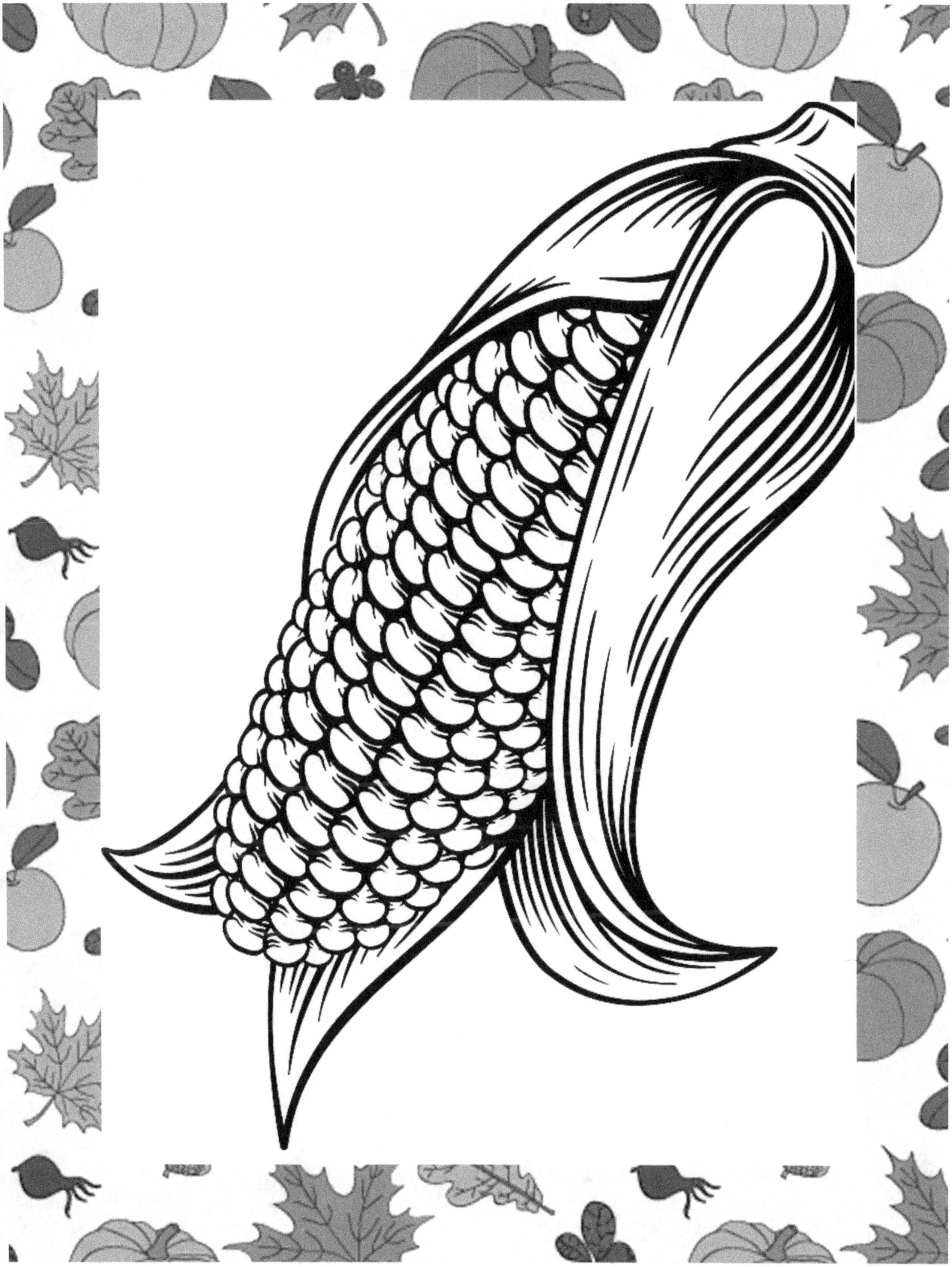

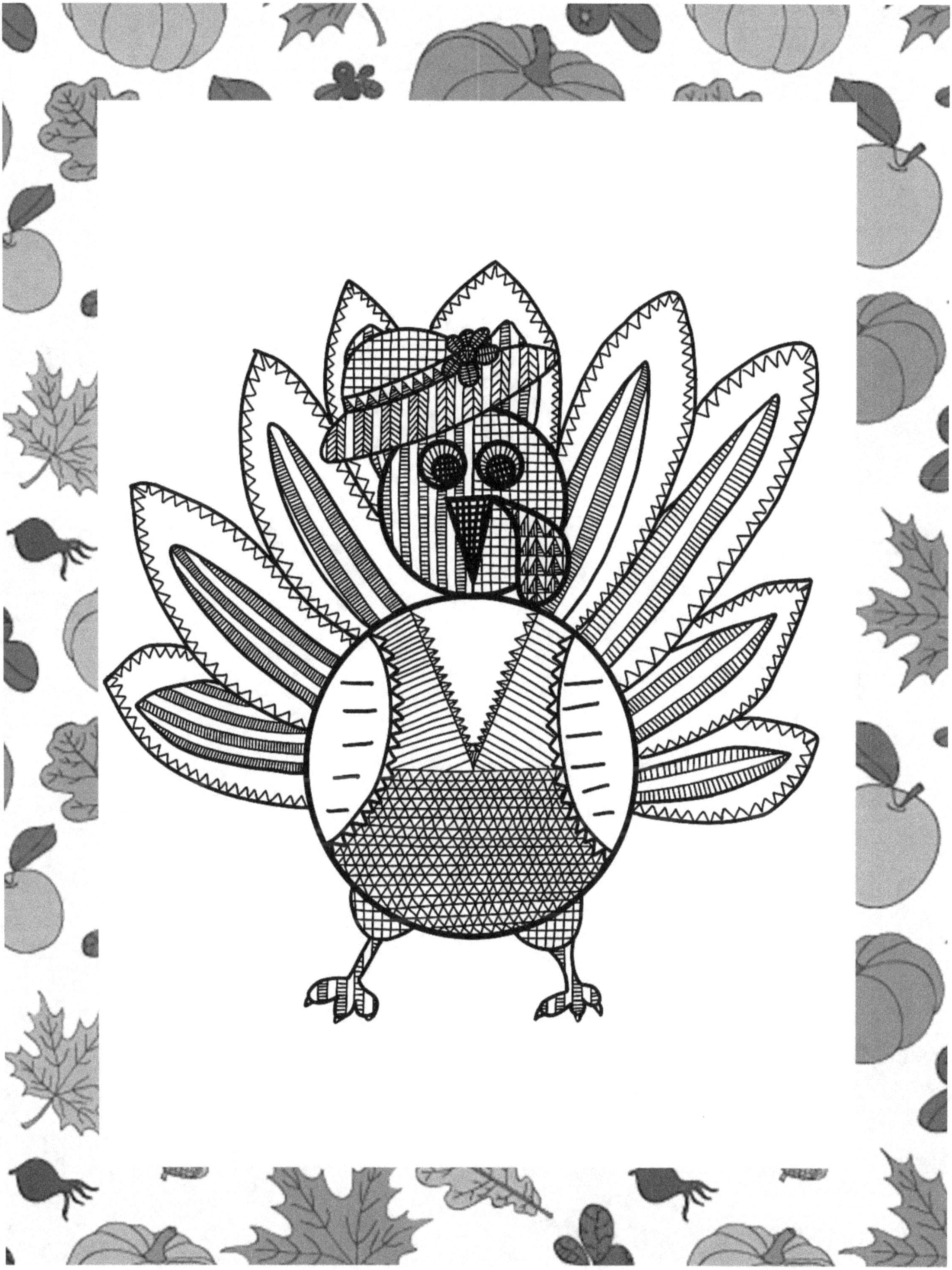

Enjoying this Notebook?

Please leave Black Rose Press House a review
because we would love to know your thought,
feedback, and opinions to create
better products for you.
*Please share how you creatively use your
notebooks and journals.*

THANKS
FOR YOUR SUPPORT

Scan This Qr Code And Visit Our
Author Page At-
amazon.com

www.ingramcontent.com/pod-product-compliance
Lightning Source LLC
Chambersburg PA
CBHW081457220526
45466CB00008B/2679